D1503274

THANK YOU FOR THE

FLOWERS AND BALLOONS

FROM HUMOR TO TUMOR AND BACK

LORI SKIPPER

DEDICATION

I dedicate this book to all my friends and family who have been there for my family and me during the good and the bad. From emotional to financial to loving support, we recognize how blessed we are to be surrounded by so many amazing people. You'll never understand how wrapped in love you've made us feel.

To my amazing husband, Stewart, you have taught me that the truly important things in life are the relationships we make and the experiences we have. You are the kind of man I hope that our son becomes and our daughter marries. I can't believe I'm lucky enough to call you mine.

To my children and biggest accomplishments, Tripp and Anna Grace, my love for you is never ending. Tripp, may you remain as compassionate, empathetic, and charming as you are today. And may you continue to treat the ladies as the princesses that they are. Anna Grace, may you forever stay as bold, charismatic, and smart as the women who came before you. Daddy and I live eternally through you both.

To my parents, Kerry and Cheri, thank you for nurturing my fun side and taking care of my sick side.

To my sister, Kasey, thank you for keeping us all on our toes, giving me much of the material for this book, and showing me so much love and support when times got hard.

And, if you're important to me but have been left out of this book, it's not because I don't love and appreciate you, or even that I don't have a hysterical anecdote to share about you. Unfortunately, now that I'm an oh-so responsible middle-aged parent, I suppose I must stay somewhat within social boundaries. Or, you got me too tipsy to remember.

Do you know anyone who lives "The Perfect Life"? From the outside looking in, Lori does. A smart, petite, attractive, athletic woman with a husband to match, and two strikingly adorable children, who, although both under six act, implausibly, like angels in public. Just wait until you get inside that unusual brain of hers. As it turns out, it's not all angels and rainbows for this inexplicably courageous lady. With a beguilingly intimate voice, in *From Humor to Tumor and Back*, Lori Skipper, *Lady Lawyer*, wife, daughter, and mother, wittily chronicles her life as a series of comedic events, despite the trials and tribulations she suffers of as an incredibly compulsive child who grows up (sort of) in South (sort of) Florida, gets through (sort of) law school, finally finds a husband, fails to get pregnant, and then finally does (sort of). We hear her upbeat attitude and see the "funny" in everything she does and in everything that happens, as she candidly tells her painful (sort of) story with insistent mirth, because *this* is who Lori is, despite the disasters and the catastrophes, the multiple miscarries, the loss of her voice (she's a lawyer, for crying out loud!), ... and the brain tumor.

Lori lives "The Perfect Life" with unadulterated passion. Unreservedly brave, unexpectedly hilarious, and inexplicably moving in her truth telling, Lori's stories will make you laugh out loud, despite that no one else can hear you. *From Humor to Tumor and Back* is a yummy, seductive treat. Read it and Lori's perfect attitude will infect you, improving your own life in the process.

— Joryn Jenkins
Attorney, Marketing Master, and Lori's First Legit Boss
Mother of an adult daughter

From one mother to another, "Thank You For the Flowers and Balloons" is a must read. Hilarious and relatable! Lori says what the rest of us are thinking but too scared to say!

— Jenni Crafton
Owner of New Tampa Fit4Mom
Mompreneur and mother to two preteen boys

Hilarious! This book absolutely oozes with Lori's personality and sly humor. Who else can make a brain tumor entertaining? Thank you for finally telling us all how to act. I am so, so proud to be your friend and. . . I'm sorry.

— The Honorable Amber Patterson
Presiding Judge, Cobb County, Georgia Juvenile Court
Mother to a 13-year-old boy and 11-year-old girl

Table of Contents

Prologue

Hi, I'm Lori. I wrote a hilarious intro to this book and then researched and learned that I could not use the actual song lyrics in my book. God, I hate lawyers, (confession, I'm a lawyer.)

So why should you care about what little ole me has to say? I'm not a social media maven. Actually the opposite; I'm the one who is always asking who else can read my comment when messaging privately with someone. Or forgetting to tag the one person the post is about. And I only do Facebook. Yes, I'll watch your hilarious TickTack videos, and my five-year-old son is addicted to SnapChat, but I can barely pin on my Pinterest board.

I know you're surprised, but I'm also not a part of the Kardashian clan (although anyone who speaks against that interesting crew should receive horrid plastic surgery or something). We ALL love them. They're like fish sticks. . . no one wants to admit it, but, come on, they're delicious. Kris Jenner for President. Make America Pretty With Awesome Asses. We'll all die in a beautiful sex orgy in under a year, but it will probably be worth it.

The truth is, unfortunately, I've got quite the story to tell, full of murder and mystery, and oh, the sex. Okay, sorry, that's a lie too. How about the truth...

My tumors are funny.

A NOTE ON SICK TUMOR HUMOR

Our family has always dealt with stress by using humor. If that doesn't sit well with you, pass this book along to a friend. Like right now.

I'll never forget the day I came home from the hospital, after just having been diagnosed with a brain tumor, and my dad kept walking around the house saying in his best Arnold Schwartzenhaeger voice, "It's naught a tuuumor." Yes, Dad, that's precisely what it is.

On the day of my first brain surgery, I sent my four-year-old to school at our Methodist church wearing shorts with skulls and crossbones all over them. You know, just for giggles.

My husband and I dressed up as a bloody brain patient and bloody surgeon for Halloween last year.

So now you know the kinda loony you're dealing with. ("With which you are dealing." See, I can write like a lawyer, I just choose not to in this tumor tome.)

**"Things work out best for those who
make the best of how things work out."**
– John Wooden

Are you a ridiculously energized person. like me, who can't sit still for too long? Can you imagine what it's like to recover from brain surgery? They won't even let me jog or do Downward Dog!

Or, are you like most of my friends and relatives who are slightly jealous that I've been forced to stop working and exercising, and encouraged to eat everything in sight? It's okay if you're one of those. Most of my favorite people are like you.

Regardless, of what drives you, I truly believe in the power of motivation to be the best you that you can be, whatever your disabilities. Heck, I'm writing a book five days after a craniotomy. I could just sit here and read someone else's book, but I'd get the same headache, so why not write my own?

Can't speak? Learn sign language. Can't hear? Get a fancy hearing aid (and only turn it on when the annoying ones aren't around you). Can barely move your body? Get you the Mercedes of wheelchairs. I have to use a walker and eye patches these days, but I always make sure there's some sort of beautiful bedazzling on them. Whatever it is, you can do this. Live your life to the fullest, even if it's no longer as full as it was or seems like less than those around you.

I know that there are a lot of "normal" people who are miserable. But why? Until you've had a major health incident, you get the luxury of being mad for stupid reasons. But once it's your health, you'll wonder what you were worried or angry about before. Don't wait until that happens. Just live kind and positive now, and don't take a day for granted.

5

Let's Start at the Very Beginning

It was a cool, crisp winter night in Fort Lauderdale, Florida. Okay, I looked it up; thank you, Farmer's Almanac. It was a balmy sixty degrees, burrrr. In true second child fashion, my mom told my dad that it was time to go to the hospital, and he requested they wait until Star Trek and his rum n' coke were finished. "Need a buzz for this baby, Honey. Just close those legs." I imagine my mom going from fits of screaming excruciating pain while a Vulcan got his wings or something, to calmly tidying up the house like the good housewife does. I recognize that this is probably a highly inaccurate rendition, but you know how stories get told throughout the years, and I wasn't on the scene yet to witness it myself.

Scene Two: The race to the hospital. In slow 5:00, South Florida traffic. Bet that was fun. I don't know if men were allowed in the delivery rooms waaaaayyyyyy back then, but they sure didn't have the penchant for staying once the baby arrived safely. Once I was born five minutes after arriving in the delivery room, my dad was whisked away by his bro crew for drinks and cigars. He was kind enough to ask my mom if she needed anything to eat, and returned hours later (okay, the next morning), smelling like a brewery, proudly waving around a sorta-fresh Philly Cheese Steak. "Congrats, Wifey, here's your celebratory street meat, extra onions!"

**"THE PROBLEM WITH THE WORLD IS THAT
THE INTELLIGENT PEOPLE ARE FULL OF DOUBTS,
WHILE THE STUPID ONES ARE FULL OF CONFIDENCE."**
- Charles Bukowski

Why is there so much hate in this world? Just be nice to people. I don't know it all. You don't know it all. So stop acting like you do, everyone. When you don't listen to other people's opinions, just waiting to make your next comeback, you look like a fool.

And when you are so apt to believe only one side of a position, you're just closing your ears to other views. How smart is that? Not very. Life ain't just black and white. It's all grey, baby. I wish it were all pink and sparkly.

Don't pick fights over your beliefs. They're your beliefs. They don't have to be mine. How much time do you spend trying to change someone's views? And sure, you may wear them down because they're sick of arguing with you. But you haven't really won them over. They just stopped listening.

The really smart individual isn't the one who yells the loudest and longest, but the one who knows when it's time to be quiet.

I AM BORN

I'm sure I enjoyed a riotous time during my first decade in Fort Lauderdale, but I don't really remember much. Here's what I do know though. . .

I was conceived on a waterbed and my sister on a boat. Hence, we are both Aquarius who enjoy the beach and eating fish. And whose parents tell them too much.

My big sister, Kasey, set the tone of our relationship early. She was the tormenter, and I, her victim. In preparation to write this memoir, I found an old I-search paper I wrote in my high school psychology class. I included pictures. The first picture shows me as a newborn, crying hysterically in my sister's arms, as she wears a shocked "I just pinched the baby" expression. I go on to explain that I would have included more

pictures in the I-search paper, but all I could find were pictures of Kasey, pictures of my dad with big fish, and pictures of my dad and Kasey holding big fish together. I further explained, "I'm not jealous of my sister. The emotion I feel mostly towards Kasey is fear." I conclude the paper noting that, "After growing up with a sister like Kasey, I am surprised that I'm still alive." I think I was going through a flare for the dramatics when I wrote that paper, but you get a general idea of our sisterly bond.

My parents were always messing with me. Not just me. Everyone, I think. But I took things very seriously, and I got to the point at a very young age where I couldn't tell if they were joking with me or telling me the truth. I would always ask, "For real and for true?" I notice I use this same funny sarcasm now with my own children. Their sense of reality is probably really skewed by me. But my five-year old does understand sarcasm now, so he's learning something from his wacky mom. As an example, when Tripp says he's scared to sleep alone in his room, I tell him that it's understandable because of the monsters under his bed. He just looks at me oddly and stares at his bed.

I've always been very accepting of others. As a very young child, I told a black woman in a checkout line that I liked the color of her tan. One of my first close friends was Rafaela, a migrant worker's daughter, who didn't speak a lick of English. This is definitely one of my qualities of which I'm most proud.

Every night, when it got dark, I called it "purple nighttime." When I would sit at a table to eat, I always demanded that my parents push me in "to my tummy, to my tummy." Aw, the beginnings of slight OCD are adorable.

When I was in preschool, I was so excited to dress up as a clown for Halloween. I looked forward to the day and made sure I had the perfect costume. When Halloween finally arrived, I happily put on my outfit. But excitement soon turned to fear when my mom insisted that she blow up balloons to put in my shirt because apparently she thought large-breasted clowns are funnier than their small-chested counterparts. I was terrified that the

balloons would burst on me and hurt me. It's either very surprising, or explains exactly, why I got breast implants years later.

I carried a security blanket for an extremely long time. (Gosh, why did I feel the need for extra security?) Once I graduated from kindergarten, my mother determined that this behavior had to stop. So, every week, my beloved blankie got smaller and smaller as my mom cut strips off of it until only one inch remained.

She really thought her OCD child would not notice. Two can play at this game, Mom. My only revenge was to continue to suck my thumb. Now I shall embarrass you and cause you enormous dental bills!

So I continued to suck my thumb. I had a strawberry-flavored thumb and a chocolate-flavored thumb. My parents tried everything to get me to stop. Gross tasting polish, weird gloves, constant annoying reminders. . . still I sucked. Finally, towards the end of kindergarten, my mom uttered the right words. "Look, if you don't suck your thumb for a week, I'll give you $20." I never sucked my thumb again. I bought a sweet Care Bear with that money. We all have our motivators.

In kindergarten, I met a young man who could see past my juvenile blankie-dragging, thumb-sucking ways. I went to his house one amazing afternoon for a play date. We played on his play set, and he kissed me under the slide. When his older twin brothers told us we were gross, we told them that they just didn't understand true love. Sadly, true love could not last the changing of elementary schools.

I ran into a lot of poles and hanging plants, like an obscene amount. Why is this? It's because of my slightly obsessive behavior of counting everything in sight. I don't think I'm autistic. My other personality traits don't really align with that diagnosis. But I'm some kind of special. So, what does this mean to the non-obsessive counter? Well, I try to limit myself as an adult, but as a kid, I counted everything. If I entered a room, I would soon know the number of blinds, wall tiles, floor tiles, whatever. If I walked, I counted steps. (Which actually helped me in my early running days because it helped pass the time, and when I was finished with a run, I'd have a good idea about my mileage or time just by knowing how high I had counted. This is my superhero power. You'd be amazed how much my secret neurosis impressed my husband early on. Maybe that's how I knew he was the one. Obsessive counting becomes running mantra. Way healthier sounding.) Anyhoo, when you count all your steps, you tend to look at your feet an inordinate amount of the time, and that makes you knock into a lot of things. I'm beginning to understand my tumors better as I write this.

One night recently, my son came to lie with me in bed and started counting all the decorative squares we have built into our ceiling. And then he counted the different shapes of them. And then the drawers. And then the blinds. I've never been so proud, and worried, in my life.

I also counted money. Like everyone's money. It's not that I cared how much they had. I just wanted it to be in a nice little pile, with all the men facing the same way, in denominations from large to small. If they were ironed and wrinkle-free, even better. What's so weird or "rude" about that?

I enjoyed, that's right, enjoyed, organizing my closet. All my outfits were in order of color, with proper accessories, on the same white hangers, all one inch away from the one before it. My sister once messed this all up in a fit of rage. Jokes on her, I loved tidying it up again. The thing is, I didn't care if other's closets were a mess, I just needed mine to be pristine. Let the tornado hit yours, but leave me be.

One more obsession I feel compelled to admit. Teaching me cursive was a bad idea. For about two years upon learning that beautiful script, every time I uttered a sentence, I also secretly

14

wrote the words with my fingers in cursive, or just imagined writing the words in my head. I knew this was weird and worked hard to break myself of it early. I mean, I had my counting, who needed letters too? I didn't want to be greedy.

My partying parents were a bit concerned about their straightedge kid. I got detention once. They high-fived each other, and my dad took me out for donuts. But these obsessions probably lead me to majoring in Psychology in college. If you can't beat 'em, join 'em!

I also had fancy taste. Surprise, surprise. While my sister gnawed on her grilled ham and cheese sandwiches and chicken nuggets, I was the five-year old at the bar (don't judge, it was a different time) ordering a dozen oysters. Raw. And no, I don't want your crackers or cocktail sauce. I want to feel that mucousy slimy goodness slide right down my throat. Maybe with a nice lemon wedge and Sauvignon Blanc. I also always wanted a white baby grand piano, though I didn't play, and a white Persian kitty, which I have now. Follow your dreams, people.

I did hate my mom's pork chops. Remember, I'm fancy and obsessive. To this day, they still taste like dry shoe soles. Give it up, Mom, you're a lovely cook, but pork chops ain't yo' thing. Stick with a nice roast chicken. Or better yet, just let Dad grill. Anyway, on this particular night, my parents promised my sister and I that they would take us out for ice cream if we ate all our dinners. Kasey dutifully ate her rank meat and stuffed her corn in the crevices of our shockingly yellow corn-colored chairs. She's the creative, don't-give-a-shit-about-anything one. I, on the other hand, could not stomach the pork. I devised a plan. I would store the remaining (all) pork in my chubby little cheek, chipmunk style. Before we left, I'd just spit it into the toilet, and receive my just reward. The only problem was that I was like five, so I didn't go to the bathroom without help. Thus I couldn't separate myself from the bland pork leather. But I wanted that ice cream. I've never seen an ice cream I could pass on. So I went to the parlor, ordered a chocolatey shake, and drank it up with that pork stored right in my cheek. Ate the whole thing. As I think about it, why weren't my parents concerned about my strange, silent demeanor or large cheek? And how did I communicate what special treat I wanted? Because ice cream is magical, I suppose. By the time I got home, I lost it, and in a sugar-induced rage, spit my nasty pork into the toilet (okay, at my mom). I'll never forget that delicious shake though.

When I was six-ish, we owned a condominium on Hutchison Island. It was a spacious penthouse suite boasting marble floors and eccentric artwork. I'm kidding. It was a 900 square feet one-bedroom condo with lots of old people and alligators around. We would spend weekends there, and my sis and I were probably the youngest people on the island. Which meant we had to entertain ourselves. Oh, boy. We definitely made up our own language and spoke nonsense whenever anyone else was around. My big sister definitely rode me around quite a bit like she was He-Man and I was her trusty pet, Battle Cat. We needed boy pals in our lives. At least for her. I would've taken a nice quiet Chinese or Indian girlfriend.

We also went to a small Lutheran elementary school and skipped down the street nightly, hand-in-hand, gaily singing Bible songs while my non-God-fearing parents cringed and bowed their heads in embarrassment. (I still don't share their religious views, but to each their own. My kids are baptized and going straight to Heaven!)

We slept on very thin "mattresses" in my parents' bedroom when we stayed at the condo. Looking back, I realize now that this is why my children still sleep in the family bed with us and are embarrassingly old for that.

But there are two condo stories that have threatened to rip a young family apart and change everything as we know it. Who pulled down the tent? And who pulled the fire alarm?

We'll start with the tent. Kasey, remember, is the mischievous one. She's also the never-diagnosed ADHD kid. Upon meeting her as an adult, a coworker's comment was, "People in this town would like to chop her up and snort her." I, I'm sure you'll recall, am the angel (perhaps with a very slight, like so slight, like barely there, dose of OCD). Plus, Kasey's got two years, and at that point, a few inches, on me. (Not anymore 4'11" sucker! I tower over you at 5'2", aka the "giant of the family.")

We had been building tents for months, trying to entertain ourselves in the condo. As a parent now, I realize how annoying this game is. Let's dirty all the sheets and make it so you can't move around anywhere in the small condo! And once you've washed them all in the public laundry room downstairs, we'll do it again!

ADHD Kasey would do most of the constructing and reconstructing when she determined she didn't like it. Young, sweet OCD Lori just wanted her sister to build a quiet place where she could read her books and play with her dolls. But over and over, day after day, Kasey would get bored just when I got comfortable and tear down the tent.

Until the day I raged. The tent came down repeatedly, as I became more upset. My mom, knowing it was Kasey's doing, said that the next one who pulled it down would get in some serious trouble. Guess what? We built an awesome tent. It could not be shaken. It was Fort Knox. Until it wasn't. Tragically, the tent fell. But who did it? The crazy older one dying for attention? Or the sweet one you'd never expect so that her sister would get in trouble? Tonight, on "Dateline."

Both my sister and I have stood by our stories that the other pulled down the tent. I certainly don't think I did, but she's also so passionate that she too didn't do it. Are either of us that diabolical? We both got in trouble.

Decades later, I have come to the conclusion that neither of us pulled down the tent. Could it be true that a six- and eight-year old are not the best tent-building engineers? Dare I say, did the tent fall on it's own? I'm sure Kasey at least had something she deserved to get in trouble for, so her punishment probably wasn't a complete waste.

But now, the fire alarm! We lived in a corner unit on the second floor, right next to that shiny red fire alarm. What kid wouldn't feel compelled to pull that? It was a Friday afternoon. I know this because we had just been grocery shopping, and my mom only shopped on Fridays. Seriously. No mid-week treats for you! She unloaded the car as Kasey and I raced upstairs. (She raced. I meandered.) She got there first. She saw her opportunity. She read "PULL." She got excited, wondering what would happen. Her fingers tingled. She wiggled them around. She stood on her toes, and she pulled that alarm with all her might.

My poor mom came running upstairs, groceries flying out of bags around her. She knew exactly who the culprit was. Mind you, I was the good one. But beyond that, I was also too short to touch the alarm and couldn't read "PULL!" However, in fair mother fashion (screw that, I would've already thrown Kasey over the ledge), she first asked for one of us to admit our wrongdoing. Kasey didn't fess up, standing there stoically. My mom, staring at two silent children, finally said, "If you don't tell me who pulled it, I'll punish you both!" And me, in true martyr fashion, burst into tears and admitted that I did it. My little utilitarian mind logically thought, "If I'm going to get in trouble regardless, why should she too?" I was way beyond my six years.

My mom kept employing this strategy of claiming she'd punish us both throughout the years, and it really didn't bode well for her or me. Kasey scored big in Mom's attempts to discipline her rambunctious child. My mom is currently staying with me now as I recover from brain and spine surgeries. We have a beautiful cat and a weird-looking dog who both feel as though they can pee wherever they please. The other day, one of the animals peed in the hallway, and I heard my mom tell them that she would punish them both if one of them didn't raise their paw and admit it was their urine. Mom, it didn't work on your kids, why would it work on the pets?

Back to the story though. Of course the fire and police departments came. Everyone was evacuated and had to stand out in the summer heat for a couple hours. But, I'm told, that the really fun part came later that evening, when the alarm short-circuited in the middle of the night. Of course, Kasey and I wouldn't know it, because we slept like babies straight through it. I bet I would've been arrested if Kasey pulled this trick today.

Oh, the early years.

Disclaimer: I eventually did get back at Kasey by telling guys she liked that she had pimples on her butt, wanted to jump their bones, and had started her period.

"IN A WORLD WHERE YOU CAN BE ANYTHING, BE KIND."
- Anonymous Sweet Individual

Don't be a mean girl or boy or whatever you are. Regina George is not cool. She may be gorgeous, but she's mean.

We need to support each other. I am not less because you are more. In fact, I'm better because I have such an accomplished friend. Why would I want to squash that?

I live a much happier life because I understand that people just need to be boosted up. As a fitness instructor for new moms, I quickly learned that many of us need this support more so than ever as we navigate through any of life's biggest changes. Why be unwelcoming to new people? Why be rude and elusive? I can't tell you how many times I've explained to friends who feel shunned by other girls that "it's them, not you." We all have our own insecurities. Even your prettiest, smartest friend may not open up to you right away because of her insecurities. You may wonder how such a goddess could have any, but we all do. And I've noticed the ones who sit highest are the least secure.

You can find something in common with anyone. Maybe she doesn't look like you. Maybe she doesn't talk like you. But maybe you share a hobby. Maybe you like the same music. Or the same food. Or admire each other's unique parenting style. Whatever it is, just start that conversation, and you'll probably discover how much you like the person. Not everyone needs to be your best friend, but I encourage you all to be everyone's friend.

If you find that you truly dislike someone, consider what you don't like about the person. Maybe she's just an awful person. Okay, there are some horrible people out there. But not many. You probably just prefer spending time with other people. That's okay and normal. But don't belittle or diminish that person just because you deem others as superior. Appreciate her for what she has to offer. You may not be her favorite person either, but it's easier to act civilly than to be a jerk. Taking the high road always has a prettier view.

I learned a valuable lesson the other day. I often get upset because strangers can be pretty inconsiderate to me when I am unable to speak loudly or clearly. Early in my sickness, my physical appearance did not show that I was sick, so strangers would be downright rude when they couldn't understand me, even though I was straining to scream to them at the top of my lungs and am physically unable to speak louder. As you can imagine, about the tenth time this happens in a day, you get kind of annoyed. So I got a bit snippy to my cashier when she was giving me a hard time for not speaking loudly. Eventually, with the kindest look in her eyes, she told me, "I'm sorry. I'm not trying to make you feel bad. I have hearing loss, and it's very difficult for me to hear anyone." I had been so focused on my own inabilities that I had failed to notice that the person across from me may have a reason for her difficulties as well. I often urge others to be more patient with people because you don't know what they're going through, and there I was, not showing the same sentiment. I apologized profusely, we exchanged a bunch of odd hand gestures, and I went on my way, reminding myself to do a better job at practicing what I preach.

SUBURBS, WE'VE ARRIVED!

We moved when I was about ten to the mean streets (clean suburbs) of Palm City, Florida.

The next segment of our story begins around 1987 when "Dirty Dancing" was all the rage. I know what you're thinking, "Why Lori, you were only a nubile eight-year old. How inappropriate!" Yes, inappropriate. And wonderful. I quickly learned a new language of getting "knocked up," learning when a female dancer is "in trouble," figuring out what it means for a man to be hit in the "Pachenga" or "ball out some little chick," and, my fave, what going "all the way" meant! I wonder now if my third grade mind actually had a clue what was really going on. Nevertheless, my friends, Kasey, and I all love, love, loved that movie. We bought the record album and sexily crawled around on the floor (elementary school style) like Baby to "Love is Strange." Totally appropriate. Thanks, Parents, for letting this one slide and for letting me rent it over and over at Blockbuster. Ever occur to you to just purchase it and save thousands? RIP Patrick Swayze.

I would be remiss if I failed to make fun of Kasey's hair during this period. Check out her beautiful bowl cut to the left. Try to disregard her amazing suspenders and Budweiser. A hairdresser actually gave her this cut. Shame on you, Hair Lady! Kasey reports that we both went to get haircuts, and she knew exactly what style she wanted, but I got to go first. And I chose an adorable shoulder-length style with cute bangs. How could I do this? That was the hairstyle Kasey wanted! (Along with every other child that age during that time.) Of course, Kasey couldn't stand the thought of looking like her little sister, so she asked the beautician to do something a little different. And the bowl cut is what they decided on. Kasey was called "Bowl Cut" from then on by the kids on the bus on into high school. See my picture to the right. This was from a different time than when Kasey got her infamous bowl cut, but I thought my perm needed to be documented.

We really weren't much of playground folks. Which is crazy to me now that I have two young children and have repeatedly visited every playground, splash pad, and pool within an hour radius of my home. My mom swears its because I always got hurt on playgrounds. Sure, blame the little one. Of course I followed my big sister up the slide and proceeded to fall off. Why was no one paying attention? I've seen my mom on a playground now with my own kids. She's not a playground mom.

Now what does a child do if she's not part of the playground crowd? She makes her own fun. One summer afternoon, my girlfriend and I found ourselves with a bit of time on our hands. Her good friends were in the process of building a new home on our street, and they were pouring the cement slabs for the seawall. Florida problems, yo. They must've just poured the clean white slabs that morning before my friend and I happened on the scene, having just had a fight with Kasey and a neighbor boy. So what did we do? Well of course, we wrote "Kasey loves James" with sticks all over the wet slabs. We thought it was hysterical. And how could we be discovered? It's not like we wrote our own names. A fun victimless crime. Except, when the family came knocking down our door looking for Kasey, who is always the culprit. She pointed her betraying finger right at our white cement-stained hands. Caught white handed! This is literally the worst thing I did as a child. I don't count the neighbor's reindeers that we made hump every Christmas or the real estate signs we took from yards to put in others. Those were merely for comedy.

There was a gorgeous Banyan tree in an empty lot of our neighborhood. It was a great climbing tree. All the neighborhood kids loved to play all over it. One Saturday afternoon, there were quite a few of us playing tag in the old tree. I was crossing a large solid branch, and one of the boys flew by me so as not to get tagged. With the grace of a walrus, I fell from the tree and sprained my elbow. It immediately blew up to the size of a grapefruit, and I couldn't move it. I ran home crying and hid in my room. My aunt and uncle were visiting from Ohio. My parents were looking forward to their fancy dinner plans, and I didn't want to ruin their good time. So I hid in my room as my elbow continued to swell, and I was in horrible pain. A couple hours later, the boy who knocked me out of the tree came to check on me. My parents had no clue what he was talking about. "What do you mean our baby is injured?" They checked on me and my very swollen arm, and we came to the agreement that they should go to their swanky dinner and take me to the hospital after. I don't like to see people miss a good time! So that's what we did.

For some time, the parents in our neighborhood had been trying to get permission to cut down the old tree. Sure enough, my injury was just what they needed. Within months, the tree was gone. Oh, and the poor boy who caused me to fall from the tree is the same boy whose name we wrote in the wet cement. This kid was constantly getting in trouble for stuff that wasn't actually his fault!

We also played in the woods, which were really just undeveloped plots of land on our street. That was great until

Kasey taunted a mean dog and got bit on the butt when we all ran away. She had to get a tetanus shot and report the dog to animal services, thus ending all of our fun times in the woods. Sorry neighborhood friends for us Kapalko girls ruining all your fun!

We were more of the "go with parents and friends to a child-friendly bar and restaurant" crowd. Get hyped up on Coco Cola and watch parents get loose on their drinks of choice. (Which btw, Dad, I always wondered why your cokes tasted sweeter and better than mine. Why would you let me sip on them? Oh, wait, I have kids, I get it.)

Of course, I won't forget the time my family and another broke in 8:00pm-late-night style (after the bar, naturally) to our elementary school's new playground with a cooler of drinks, and my dad and his friends left open beers all over for the kindergarteners to enjoy when they arrived at recess on Monday morning.

Our family also broke into the hotel pool after hours in Williamsburg. Looking back, this is not such a risky adventure. But at the time, my little eleven-year-old self couldn't believe that we were breaking such rules. And we did eventually get kicked out by security because we were naughty people! But, oh, the cannonball dives we enjoyed until then!

I believe on the same vacation, on our long journey to see my aunt and uncle in Ohio, we had to drive through Jacksonville 5:00 traffic. My dad was super stressed out by it, as he tends to get. So to ease the mood in the car, Kasey and I decided to make posters that read "HONK IF YOU'RE HORNY" and place them in our rear windows. I'm pretty sure I had no clue what this even meant, but boy, did we get a reaction. Every semi-truck on the highway was honking at my dad, and he had no clue what was going on. My sister and I were in hysterics. My dad was flabbergasted as to what he was doing wrong, causing all these professional drivers to honk at him. I think my mom eventually caught on and couldn't keep a straight face. Finally the jig was up, and Dad ordered us to sit still (including Mom) and be quiet until we got to Georgia.

When we did finally arrive in Ohio, my mom asked me how I liked it, and I responded, "It's nice, I suppose, but they don't take good care of their trees." I guess their leaves don't just grow and flourish all year 'round like ours do. The pictures of the trip are quite lovely though. In my preteen photo album, I have each picture labeled, including who is in  the picture. As though years from then, I would forget who my aunt or mother is. Again, slight OCD, what can you do?

I believe on the same vacation (this must've been an epic trip, or else, my parents learned their lesson and didn't take us anywhere else again), we went to Dollywood. Not surprisingly, Kasey was the risk taker who wanted to go on all the roller coasters with my dad. My mom had wisely instilled in me at a young age that I would always be too small for roller coasters, that they would be the death of me if I road one, and that I should sit patiently with her while we waited for Kasey and Dad's raucous entertainment. Mom had apparently felt like she was gong to fall out of a wooden roller coaster at a young age, and I was the willing child who she scared into watching the fun from the sidelines.

There was one ride that didn't seem so bad, so the entire family decided to give it a try. It seemed to be slow enough and was just like a boat ride in the tranquil water. What we did not realize until it was too late was that it was actually a flume ride that ended in a steep plunge to your probable death, whilst soaking you in the process. As we hit the precipice of the decline and dangled over the edge, I screamed to my mother, "I don't want to do this! Get me out!" To which my mom encouragingly responded, "I don't either! What the f*ck do you want me to do about it now?!" And down we went. We did survive to see more of Dollywood, but it was a long time before I could ride a coaster again. And I don't think I ever really trusted my parents after that.

This fear escalated to my fear of Ferris wheels. Yes, most find them peaceful, as they slowly glide around the sky providing majestic scenes of the landscape for miles. Not me. I was terrified. When I was about ten-years old, we went to the county fair. In an attempt to get me to ride the slow, huge wheel, my parents started me on the small kids' wheel. But this one was fast! Or at least to me it was. As I watched numerous five-year olds gleefully love the experience, I waited my turn. I got on with my sister, got strapped in, and off we went. As soon as we hit the top, I was screaming. "Get me off this thing! I don't like it! Why are you doing this to me?!" My parents thought I should go around one more time because maybe I'd start to enjoy it. I did not. They had to stop and let me off so that much younger fairgoers could jump on. Kasey just cringed.

The funny thing is that, as an adult, I absolutely love roller coasters. I would go alone to a theme park just to ride them. Stewart gets motion sick, so he's not much of a companion on the wild rides. But I adore them. I even skydived in college, after which, I called my parents to tell them what I had just survived. They couldn't believe that I had just jumped out of a perfectly good plane. (It actually wasn't a perfectly good plane. Jumping out of it was probably the safer choice than landing in it.)

While we're on the topic of family vacations, can we discuss how my biggest, most family-packed vacation was as a third grader in Vegas? Because why wouldn't it make sense to take two elementary-aged children, along with their grandparents and uncle to Las Vegas? But we did! I'm beginning to realize that my childhood resembled the Griswolds'. We all flew across the country where we stayed at Circus Circus Hotel and Casino. It had a circus theme, so surely it was appropriate for a young family. My sister and I got let loose in the upstairs "children's casino" while the adults gambled below. Can you imagine letting your eight- and ten- year olds loose in a casino these days? Honestly, we had a blast. We saw "Siegfried & Roy," and my parents made me ask them if I could "pet their pussy." I did not understand why this was so funny. I also learned some poker skills, enough to beat my very experienced grandpa at penny poker. Badly. He vowed to never play with me again. We also saw the Grand Canyon and the damn dam, but those didn't make quite as much of an impact as the casino.

I'm not Jewish, but I lived in South Florida, so I watched more young Jewish children become men and women at lavish parties than I can shake a chuppah at. My best friend for years was Nikki (now Niki, we needed a change). Niki is the girl, and comes from the family, we all want our kids to be around. Well, there was that time her dad went to prison, but it was all white-collar crime related, so we continued to adore and respect him. He learned Spanish and basket weaving at his halfway house.

Check out our very similar eight-grade Class Night dresses in the photo above. Aren't they breathtaking in all their squishy, sparkly gloriousness? And notice how well I coordinated my heels by dying them to match perfectly! And the hair and makeup! More is better!

Niki was so good, I was the bad one. How fun! I did things like practice psychology on their cat and eat all their food. She did things like make her brilliant brother do my science fair projects. I helped her learn her Jewish prayers for her Bat Mitzvah. "Baruch haba b'shem adonai," see, I still got it! (I also know all the presidents in order and all the states in alphabetical order. Don't challenge me, you will not succeed.) I think the worst thing I ever made Niki do was drink her mom's Manischewitz and replace it with a concoction of vanilla extract and water. Sorry, Sharon!

To say that I lived a sheltered life is an understatement. My friends and I were obsessed with Garth Brooks. When he came to Miami, we just had to see his concert. So my mom and Niki's mom drove us down for the show of a lifetime. We saw bums! And rode a big city metrorail! Of course, I sat on the floor of the train because I was concerned by the idea of drive-by shootings.

27

Looking back, sitting on the floor of a Miami metrorail is much more frightening.

My dad owned his business as a dental technician, and my mom did the books for it. Around this time, she gave me the task of writing statements. This is where you handwrite each monthly invoice for each dentist showing all the crowns, bridges, and other teeth stuff you made for them. Remember, this was a long time ago. No, we did not have a computer program to make this job a lot simpler. Surprisingly, the dentists knew as soon as I took over the position. Because I made a lot of mistakes? No, none, who are we discussing here? I suppose it may have been because I drew little hearts over every "i." The next month, to keep my highly competitive secretarial position, I had to agree to draw bubbly circles instead of hearts. Let's be serious, Kasey did not want this chore, so I didn't have to negotiate with my mom too much.

When I was in middle school, I became a cheerleader. I loved it. I'm the small one, so we experimented new stunts on me a lot. Again, how could I have gotten a brain tumor? I was only dropped on my head repeatedly as it developed. Hmmmm. But I loved the activity and the relationships. I love having girlfriends. Embrace this women. . . there is no support like that of an awesome group of women around you. We're pretty much all nurturers, so we just nurture each other until we can't stand it. It's beautiful.

My two best friends were also cheerleaders, Dena and Chrissy. Dena, wait for it, was the daughter from the family whose seawall I tried to destroy. I guess you do get a second chance to make a first impression. Chrissy comes from a family with seven kids, and they have always been the most kind, accepting people. I have no doubt that I hold some of my "love everyone" views today based on what I learned from her family way back when. We were good kids. Our biggest mishap occurred when we were designing cheer buckets for younger cheerleaders, and we were trying to open a glitter paint pen to no avail. We finally got that sucker open, spraying gold glitter paint all over my kitchen wall. My parents (Dad especially, I blame you for my OCD) were neat freaks, so we could not have this. We tried to clean it up with cleaners and paper towels, of course, spreading the mess bigger. Never fear! Dena's dad was in the painting business, and he surely had some white paint in the garage at home. She quickly biked home and took just what we thought we needed. We would just paint over the glitter, and no one would ever be the wiser that the wall was different shades of white and smelled like fresh paint. Except Dena took shiny baseboard paint instead of flat wall paint. About the time we discovered our issue, my parents arrived home. What do  you do? We all ran with our supplies and locked ourselves in my bathroom, in the shower no less, and listened as they tried to figure out "what the hell happened." They finally discovered us hiding in the bathroom, and I think just thought it was funny because we really weren't doing anything wrong, tried our best to fix it, and the problem wasn't really a tough one for a dad to fix anyway. We were like Lucy, Ethel, and a spare Ethel in "I Love Lucy."

We also hosted all the cheerleader sleepovers at our house. My sister was a cheerleader too, so there were a lot of girls running around all the time, especially around high school age. We ranged from girls like me (is she ten?) to girls like my friend, Melissa (she must be twenty). Looking back, I always think it's funny to imagine my fifty-year-old father amongst all these beautiful near-naked girls. Because cheerleaders never wear clothes. (Why do we do this?) He would hide from us a lot, only to come out early in the morning, bang pots together over all the sleeping beauties, and make everyone breakfast. He definitely got an eye-full once when Melissa ran out to moon Kasey and accidentally mooned my parents. We refer to her as "Moony Mel" to this day.

I was also on the debate team, which looking back, I hated. Why did I become a lawyer again? I felt like all my debate friends were constantly telling "This one time, at debate camp" stories. I would prepare for competitions with my parents before dinner when we'd have discussions about what I should write about, and then, bam, it would hit me. My dad says to this day that you should never deliberately teach a teenager how to argue. . . his biggest parenting fail. I did make it to nationals in oratory and made poor Niki drink wine with me in our room. I have no memory of how we accomplished this great feat, but I think we got caught and I blamed it on being distraught from having just witnessed the beautiful giraffes shackled to cement slabs at the Kansas Zoo.

My husband played drums in the marching band in high school. He swears that at his school, the band kids were cool and the cheerleaders were not so popular. Um, no, I went to a high school like any other where the cheerleaders and athletes were cool, and the debate and band people were dorks. Note, I married one of you band dorks and was a debate nerd myself, so I'm allowed to make this joke.

Let's discuss boobs now and the fact that I had none until I bought myself a pair in law school. Can I tell you about an amazing product for small-chested women of the nineties? The water bra! Yes, it is a padded bra, but instead of padding, it's filled with water to feel more lifelike. Genius! I recall purchasing my first water bra. I made my mom come with me so that she could hug me and touch me and make sure my boobs felt legit. I also remember later having to have serious conversations with new boyfriends before our relations became too intimate to let them know that my boobs were actually water, and not the gorgeous specimens they appeared to be. Of course, when I later had my breast augmentation, I handed down my coveted water bras to my less fortunate chested friends. Lori, always the giver.

I had two jobs in high school. I was a yogurt squirter and then an ice cream scooper. My first job was at the yogurt shop. I loved it. All my girlfriends worked there, and my boyfriend worked at the Publix next door. I got all the free yogurt I could handle. Unfortunately, this dream only lasted a year before the yogurt shop went under. I knew trouble was lurking when I came to work and they didn't have vanilla or chocolate yogurt left. So what did we do with our unemployment? My friends and I all got jobs at the ice cream parlor. Again, this gig lasted about a year before going under. Curiously, I worked at a bagel shop in college, and this restaurant too went belly up after about a year. Moral of the story, don't hire employees who eat all your product.

My middle-upper class upbringing included a new Mustang when I reached the very mature age of sixteen. Kasey chose a used Honda Civic for her first car instead. Told you I was the fancy one. The most fun we had in high school was driving (our own!) boats to the sandbars every weekend to get loopy and loose on hunch punch. We were just preparing our young bodies for college.

I met my adorable high school boyfriend, Jeremy, right when I started high school. He was a year older and had met my crazy Kasey when they bagged groceries together at Publix. I think he probably started with a crush on her and then realized there was a younger, sweeter model. We dated all through high school. We had great times together. He and his family treated me like a princess. There isn't a bad thing to say about him. I'm trying to think of a funny story to tell about the Jeremy years, but the good stuff really all involves first sexual experiences and what not. I mean, check out that photo above of me giving him that "come and get this sexy barely pubescent fifteen-year old." I'm pretty sure my mother took this pic.

Oh, I got a story. Jeremy has a massive member. And I had never seen one before, so I thought they were all that big. They're not. His family should all be very proud of him. Oh, and we had sex in his parents' bed. We were drunk on White Russians. Parents, this will happen to all our beds eventually. Just embrace it, and wash your sheets often. After four romantic years, I maturely

dumped him as I drove away to college at The University of Florida. Go Gators! Why aren't the men's privates as big as they were in high school?

"LET THE KIDS RUN AS FAST AS THEY CAN TODAY COZ LIFE WILL RUN FASTER THAN KIDS WHEN CHILDHOOD IS OVER."
- Kumar Aakash

I know it's hard as a parent to let your kids just be kids. It can be annoying. And tiring. But they're basically learning everything from the ground up. And for a while, they can't even communicate. I certainly now understand how frustrating that is and would like to throw myself on the floor and kick around in a fit of rage once in awhile (everyday).

If you're concerned about your kids, you're doing a great job. You care. You will make sure that they become the best people they can be. Don't compare yourself, or your kids, or your marriage, to others'. We all have our obstacles. Nobody's life is perfect, despite how fabulous it looks on social media. I'm sitting here right now unable to smile because of the paralysis in my face. But my kids are beautiful, and my husband's gorgeous, so I post great pictures of them. Someone from the outside would think that I live a marveled life. You never know what's on the other side of that camera.

Let the kids be kids, and support everyone's families, whether you agree with their decisions or not. My very best friend, Michelle, raises her kids way differently than me. She never tried to breastfeed; I can't get my 20-month old off my boob. She signed up for elective C-sections; I tried for a natural birth. Her kids slept in their own rooms at like four-months old. We either sleep all snuggled up in the family bed, or I sleep with the baby, and my husband sleeps with our five-year old. But it doesn't matter. Michelle's a great mom. I'm a great mom. We're just different kinds of moms. I love that my kids are comfortable going to her house

33

and experiencing their fun times, and I love that her kids can come to my house and not touch my stuff. Just kidding. Sorta.

I could very easily have met her once I already had kids and dismissed her parenting views as too different from mine. And then my family would've missed out on sharing life with this amazing family.

Let the kids be kids. Let the parents be parents. And let them all be your friends.

"A" IS FOR ANNBITION

My Middle Name is "Ambition." Okay, it's "Ann," but they both start with an "A." Annbition?

I was recently looking at old school records from when I was just four-years old. While I was above average in most things, the only subject I actually excelled in was my "ambition." It's amazing how these things are ingrained in you at an early age. It's just who I am.

When my gymnastically talented sister did a flip on the couch, I just knew I could do it, too. I could not. I rolled right off that couch into our new pointy glass table, cracking my head open, and requiring a trip to the hospital and stitches. The scar looks cool to this day. I guess couch tumbling is ambitious for a three-year old.

When my sister got a bike with no training wheels for her sixth birthday, I immediately asked my dad where mine was. I just knew I could do it, too. I wasn't even four yet. (Okay, so I turned four two days later, but who's counting?) Note to parents of young children: Don't take them on family bike rides where you get to ride your big huge bikes, and the youngest one is stuck on her dinky pink little bike. Can you imagine how much effort it takes for her to keep up?

You know how there are those "mom phrases" that just stick with you for life? My mom used to always tell Kasey and me to not do things "half-assed." Very appropriate advice for preteens, Mom. Looking back, what did she even mean? Maybe it was good advice for Kasey, but I've never done a thing in my life "half-assed." I put my whole ass into everything I do.

My mom used to always tell people that she never had to push me because I was my toughest motivator. I remember at a very young age asking my teachers everyday if there was anything I needed to do to prepare for the next day. I was always looking ahead and wanting to be prepared. And kind of anal and annoying, I suppose.

I don't think I was the smartest student. But I was always the hardest worker. And that will get you far. You can have all the talents in the world, but if you lack the ambition, you won't go far. Me, on the other hand, was born to push myself to my limits. In school, I rarely received a grade that wasn't an "A." I always took upper level classes. I studied for the LSAT, not because I wanted to be a lawyer, but because I wanted the challenge. That's kinda the reason I went to law school too. I didn't ever have a burning desire to change the world through my jurisprudence. I just wanted the challenge of becoming an attorney.

I worked as a lawyer at a small law firm for about twelve years before I had my first baby. I was going to go back after maternity leave, but who were we kidding? Everyone knew I was going to stay home with my baby. When my husband was laid off when our son was just three-months old, we were suddenly faced with the scary reality of no income. For a couple of successful professionals, this was terrifying.

So I started my law firm. I started small and stayed small. But in no time, I was earning more than I ever had working for a firm.

"KEEP AWAY FROM PEOPLE WHO TRY TO DWINDLE YOUR AMBITIONS. SMALL PEOPLE ALWAYS DO THAT, BUT THE REALLY GREAT MAKE YOU FEEL THAT YOU, TOO, CAN BECOME GREAT."
- Mark Twain

Remember, people who squash your ambitions are most likely just poorly handling their own insecurities. It's not about you; it's about them. Don't let anyone put out your flame. Surround yourself with people who ignite it. We all have something to offer.

Be a mentor. There are others in all walks of life who can learn from you. Give yourself to others. Offer your guidance and encouragement. A lot of us just need a bit of support to become so much better than who we already are.

Let yourself be mentored by others. I don't care how much you think you know, how experienced you are, or your age. We can all learn from those around us. Don't consider yourself too whatever to continue to learn your entire life.

Be ambitious. Whatever it is. Do you want to excel in your career? Go to all those work functions. Join those committees. Go to important conventions and seminars. Participate. Learn. Get your name out there.

Trying to lose weight? Put down that cookie. "But I'm hungry." So eat an apple. Take thyself to the gym. "But my back hurts." Work on your arms and legs (never mind that your back probably hurts because you don't move it enough). You can make an excuse why you can't do anything, or you can just shutty your face and do it. You may actually start to like it.

Wanna be the most awesome parent? Take more time to connect with your kids. (Btw, mine is currently screaming in my ear and kneeing me in the arm. Take mine too.)

The point is, be ambitious in whatever is important to you. We all have room for improvement.

THE POOP CHRONICLES

So, I've always known that I've had a book in me to write. Although, I never would've imagined it to be on the current subject. Here's what I envisioned. . . .

"The Poop Chronicles" – a tale of living and letting go, by Yours Truly.

Ta da!!!! Plop.

The idea began about twenty years ago when my love for long-distance running really took root in college. If you've ever been a runner, you understand the importance that poop takes on in your life. I can't say I'm proud of all the times that I've literally run the shit out of me on the side of the public road, in my community entrance, under a bridge, etc. Okay maybe I'm a little proud I ran that much. Or maybe I should just stop drinking coffee right before I tie the laces.

Anyhoo, my hilarious poop stories segued into learning about my friends and relatives' obnoxious poo stories. I mean, when someone realizes she has an outlet for a poo tale, my, is she eager to share. It would always end with a "So, have I made it into your book?"

I soon realized that pooping is not just for runners. It's for us all. Cue patriotic music and poop emojis. I picture a chapter for each major pooing occurrence. Of course this includes when you're sick, but what about when it happens on the first date? Or when you first move in with people of the opposite sex? And then when a woman gets pregnant, and is so constipated from all the hormones, and then suddenly not during the bathtub homebirth? And baby poop, I don't even need to mention the hilarities that ensue there. Try potty training. We have a couch that we literally

39

refer to as the "poop couch" because our son pooped there, right on the couch, for like three months. (Don't sit on our upstairs couch.)

So, I've got a lot of ideas for a toilet room book that you can read while you're relieving yourself. And I really hope you like me by the end of this first book, so don't steal my idea before I write it.

You know what, on second thought, if you have a poop book in you too, write it. I'll go on tour with you and my poop book, and we'll christen this country by defecating all over it. Everyone has their own unique poop tale to tell. You tell yours!

"Those who teach the most about humanity aren't always human."
- Donald L. Hicks

I've always been a pet person. Honestly, when I hear that someone is not, I kind of judge her just a little. I know it mainly has to do with your upbringing. Generally, if you were raised with pets, you want pets when you grow up. I was raised with a dog and cat. So to me, a home is not really a home unless a dog greets you at the door, and a cat ignores you. I won't lie, they do annoy me a bit. But all family does, right?

I also wonder about people who truly treat their pets like children. Like to the extreme. Do animals really need their own spa and acupuncturist? Or if they're sick or injured, at what limit is the expense to fix them too high? Does your cat need to ride around outside in a stroller? Does your dog really need filtered water? Do you post too many pictures of them on Facebook? I know I post constant pictures of my children, but they're real live people who change at a dramatic pace and do adorable things like falling off rocking horses and cutting their own hair.

My parents and sister are a bit of pet lovers to the extreme. My sister has every kind of pet you can imagine from dogs to chickens to bunnies to fish to guinea pigs, you name it, she has it. She even domesticated a possum recently. She thought it was so cute. No, Kasey, it was disgusting. And she's constantly rescuing animals, even wild birds of prey, and holding random snakes and other disgusting creatures.

When my parent's beloved Tiki died (the college dropout cat you'll hear about shortly), they were adamant that they didn't want another animal because they didn't want to care for one or have to worry about one when they traveled. I told them constantly that they really needed to just get another cat, and they ignored me. And now they have three mountain kitties living with them. They just couldn't understand why these three stray cats kept coming back to their house (even though they kept leaving food and water out for them). Finally, they were able to capture them all and have them neutered, lest they spread their seed to other mountain kitties.

They only allow "the chosen one" inside. Yes, this is what they call him. It started when my mom was out of town. My dad started to let Scamp (another one of his names) in the house, but only on Tiki's old scratching post. Dad would just move Scamp through the house on the post. This worked for a few weeks. Now Scamp comes in the house at his leisure and sits wherever he damn well pleases. So he's an outdoor/indoor cat, which I don't quite understand because I think we've already established that I don't do things "half-assed." The other two strays just stay outside on the patio and eat all the food. For some reason, I do understand this.

And here's a pet story that doesn't include me, but my mother insisted that I share. Before I was born, my parents had an Irish Setter named "Princess." Princess was quite the lovely specimen, so my newlywed parents wanted to share her offspring with the world. They found a purebred male Irish Setter and invited him to the house for a weekend rendezvous with their untouched virginal princess. And they waited. And creepily followed the two dogs around. But no puppy penetration occurred. So my parents, up for any challenge, decided to show the dogs exactly how you do it "doggy style." Apparently my folks don't know the correct way either because the dogs still refused. My mother assures me that no puppies or children were conceived during this process. She also once told me when I was in high school that our dog always watched my parents being intimate. I'll never get over that thought.

Back to my point; I think I started with one. Some of us are cat people, some are dog people, some are "all the pets" people, and some are "none of the pets" people. Whatever you are, and whatever brings you happiness, be that person. And if you wanna have your picture taken with your cat and Santa on Christmas and post it all over social media, who are we to judge?

To All the Pets I've Loved Before, Some More Than Others

I grew up with two cherished pets, an Irish Setter named Pepper, and a Himalayan kitty named Marshmallow. Pepper was a really incredible dog. When she was only a few weeks old, she became very ill, and my parents spent gobs of money to have the vet save her life. We think that she always knew and was forever grateful, so she took extra good care of us.  Every night, at the end of dinner, this fifty-pound dog would get on my mom's lap and finish whatever was left on her plate. Whenever we had company over, my mom would say, "She never does this!" And, Pepper knew that she wasn't allowed to sit on the couch. So if you were sitting on the couch, she would get on top of you and lift her limbs and tale so that no part of her touched the couch. Technically, she was not breaking any rules.

 Marshmallow was deemed to be a purebred by the pet store, but let's be honest, she was not. I don't know what the heck she was, and she sure didn't look like a marshmallow. More like a very burnt one. When we were young, we tortured her by pretending she was our baby by putting her in doll clothes, cribs, and strollers. Wisely, she soon learned to hide under the bed from us, where she remained for decades, only to come out for feedings. This lack of

45

movement caused her to balloon to an astronomical size of about 25-pounds. When she walked, her belly rubbed on the ground. So she didn't walk much.

When I went to college, I needed a pet. And I had a cool looking empty (of course) Parrot Bay bottle that I thought a fish would look neat in. So I bought a betta fish, shoved him in his bottle, and named him "Rummy." What a cool decoration. Except I couldn't really get him out to clean the bottle. But did you know, betta fish can live for years consuming their own filth? I didn't even really need to feed him that much because his "tank" was so nasty. He kinda became a little science experiment. There was one day I came home from class, and Rummy was floating belly up. But I wasn't ready yet to send him to that toilet bowl in the sky, so I sprinkled some more food in his bottle and went out with my friends. When I returned, he was swimming around as though nothing had happened. Rummy finally met his hard-earned demise when I moved from my townhome to a house in August Gainesville heat. I may have packed his bottle in the very center of my car (to keep him safe and ensure that his bottle didn't spill), and then forgotten that he was there until I unpacked the rest of the car. Let's just say that there were fish guts everywhere by the time I got to him. I really don't know what happened because it was like he exploded. Perhaps the water got so hot and boiled, thus blowing him to smitherines? I have no idea if this is a feasible possibility, but that's what it looked like.

I also bought a beautiful purebred Himalayan cat named "Tiki" in college. Actually, in true college fashion, his full name was "Tequila." He ate pizza and enjoyed the smell of weed. My drunk roomies once painted him blue. He was like the mascot of our house. Until he got kicked out of college. Our landlord wouldn't let a stoner kitty stay, so he was sent to my parents. I tried to get him back several times with no luck. He was now living the spoiled kitty life he deserved. How quickly we forget our pizza upbringings when we finally taste steak.

When I got my first big girl law job, my boss couldn't imagine me living alone with no pet. So, she got me a guinea pig. I hate rodents of any kind. I don't care how cute they think they are. Even squirrels are just rats with better outfits. But this was my new boss, so I had to pretend that this was the best gift ever. I think I named him something generic like "Wilbur." I took him home and kept him for about three weeks. My boss remembers it to only have been overnight, but trust me I know. Because I spent those three weeks terrified. You see, guinea pigs are nocturnal. They make most of their weird noises at night. I was a girl, living alone in a new apartment in my first big city. And now I had an animal making odd noises all throughout the night while I tried to sleep. I'd wake up each night terrified that there was an intruder there to get me. Thankfully, it was just stinky Wilbur. But how long could I live in fear like this? One of my friends visited often, so he cleaned the cage for me, because I could barely stand touching Wilbur. I finally walked into work one day, rodent tank in hand, and told my boss that I just couldn't take it any longer!

A couple of years later, I decided that I was mature enough for my own pet. I really wanted a teacup yorkie, and my boss even agreed that I could bring him with me to work everyday. So it actually seemed like a better idea than getting a cat. I got Rocky from an uppity breeder (Spanish dude whose house smelled like urine), and I was immediately enamored. He only grew to be four adorable pounds. I took Rocky everywhere in the fashionable bag I bought for him. I made him wear cute outfits. I loved him. The only problem is that small dogs are very difficult to potty train. Try as I might, I was having little luck, and my apartment was beginning to smell. Rocky was also very protective of me. So when I'd spend my time with another man, he would just bark his head off if we got close. I soon learned that Rocky was really impinging on my single-girl fun. When someone offered to purchase him, I sadly agreed, understanding that sometimes the strongest thing to do is let go.

A few years later, I had another itching for a pet. But this time I knew that it should be a cat and not a dog. And I didn't have a lot of money (or any), so I went the route of adopting a free kitty. Tinkerbelle was your average orange tabby with an undersized head and oversized hips.

When Stewart and I moved into our first house together, we went on a brief vacation to a friend's house in Texas. Unbeknownst to us, our declawed, not too bright, Tinkerbelle, made her way outside the house as we were packing the car for our trip. When we returned a few days later, I knew something was immediately wrong when all her food remained and her litter was fecal-free. Stewart was convinced  she had died in the house somewhere, but she wasn't old and had been showing no signs of sickness. We searched the neighborhood with no luck. I put up signs, but the only responses we received were child pranksters calling late night to leave messages, saying in sinister voices, "We got your kitty" and laughing hysterically. This might upset some, but Stewart and I would just laugh each time, knowing we probably would have done the same thing when we were young. After about a month of her missing, we pretty much gave up hope. And then, as we were packing to leave for a cruise, my neighbor came by to tell me that he thought he found my cat. Sure enough, she was stuck in the gutter next to our house! We lured her out with food, and my once plump kitty was skin and bones. She had clearly been attacked by hood cats because she had deep scratches all over her. What did we do? We had places to be. I washed her, and we left her with a bunch of food in the house as we cruised away. I imagine she was ready for some peace and quiet. When we returned, she was still alive, but now with a new nickname, "Gutter Kitty!"

 My husband brought a dog into our relationship. No, not a manly Labrador or German Shepherd. Bailey is a small black Chihuahua. And not Stewart's first Chihuahua. Apparently he had two others, Jäger and Kahlúa, in college. Before I had kids, Bailey was my kid. She came to work with me everyday. I carried her around in a sling. I made her run with me. We did six miles together one day, and she just kept

going! She started to no longer represent a fat tootsie roll. I even wanted her to be my ring bearer in our wedding, but I was quickly convinced that was a bad idea.

And then I had my own real live baby. Bailey began to get ignored, and it stressed her so much that she licked all her hair off and regained her hard-earned weight loss. She's never snapped at any children, she's just a little irritated that they've taken her place.

Side note to neighbors who post all over the neighborhood Facebook pages pictures of dogs pooping in their yards, I just want to go to your house and poop in your yard myself. My dog has actually not done this in our new neighborhood, but I know she has in the past. However, she's small, and poops the size of a squirrel poo. Does it really matter if she escapes out the front door one time and poops in your yard when I'm trying to get my two young children out of their car seats and safely into the house? Get a real problem, people.

Back to Bailey. She has an under bite. Her entire lower jaw juts out really far, and it's an interesting look, to say the least. Her mouth started to really smell badly, so I finally had the vet clean her teeth. She lost 24. Now before you judge me about my dog parenting skills, did you know that dogs have 42 teeth? So she had a lot left, and her eating habits have not changed. The vet admonished me saying that they only had to extract two because the rest just fell out on their own when the vet cleaned the plaque away. Saved me some money on those extractions, good doggy. Needless to say, her breath improved greatly, and her grin got even weirder because now just her canines protrude since the rest are missing.

Around the time I got sick, we had to put down Gutter Kitty. Eventually, I determined that, I am and always have been, more of a cat person than a dog person. Dog people always seem cooler, but I can't deny it any longer. My name is Lori, and I prefer cats. Think about it. You go to someone's house, and their dogs jump all over you and smell your crotch, as you repeatedly say that "it's okay" and push the dogs away. Go to a cat owner's house, and you probably won't even see the cat unless she's snootily walking away with her tail high. I prefer that. I say now that my cat is my favorite member of the family because she really doesn't demand much from me.

So when I really started to not feel well, I began searching for overpriced kitties to buy. I searched all over the country, but when I found a seven-week old white Persian living only a city away, I knew this was the luxurious kitty for me. Because we got her the weekend COVID quarantine started, we named her Coco Rona. We call her Coco, and she's a total gorgeous diva. Tripp loves her like I do. We always discuss how pretty she is. Anna Grace carries her around like a doll, and Coco allows it. She even matches our house.

**"A MAN'S MIND, STRETCHED BY NEW IDEAS,
MAY NEVER RETURN TO IT'S ORIGINAL DIMENSIONS."**
- Oliver Wendell Holmes Jr.

Education is an amazing gift. And I don't mean that we all need to go to college. We don't, and a lot of us shouldn't. Honestly, I'm an advocate for apprenticeships and internships. Even when you're becoming a big, bad, scary lawyer, you learn everything in your first job, once you've left law school. Most higher education is really just being hazed by your elders and jumping through hoops. If the ones before us make it hard enough to achieve, they'll weed a bunch of us out.

Don't let others be intimidating. Be whatever you want to be. Maybe the military is for you. Maybe trade school. Maybe college. Maybe grad school. Maybe you're perfectly content skipping school after high school and raising a passel of kids. That's cool too.

Just do what you want to do. Don't let anyone tell you that you can't. I have a friend with whom I went to law school who didn't actually get admitted right away. He was on the wait list, fairly low down. But he really wanted to go to my law school. So he bothered admissions everyday until he annoyed them so much that he actually got in! And now, he's probably the most successful lawyer we know. If you want something that strongly, you're going to be good at it.

If you want to badly enough, you can and will, no matter your upbringing (says the girl who had a shiny new Mustang on her sixteenth birthday, I get it, but I'm serious).

"ONE FUNNY THING ABOUT COLLEGE IS THAT TEACHERS MAKE YOU SLEEP DURING THE DAY, AND FRIENDS DON'T LET YOU SLEEP AT NIGHT."
- Anonymous College Graduate

Disclaimer: During my years from college to marriage, admittedly, I had some fun and wild times. I don't hold much back here because what's the point? These are hilarious stories, and I made it out alive. I am now a professional, mature mother of two who sits on her son's preschool church school board. I go to church, am involved in my community, perform in athletic events, and do all the responsible grown-up stuff. My point is, don't judge me by these next chapters. Or skip them, and miss the real funny stuff. Some of the names have been changed to protect my now very professional friends. I will tell you that most of my friends are hoping that I publish a naughty version of this book next. So, yes, I suppose I have held back those really good gems. But, I'm sure you'll enjoy the following almost as much!

I remember standing in the driveway, about to drive away to college, and my dad giving me his sage advice: "Learn what you can, but mostly, have fun." I think he graduated from Animal House University. Don't worry, Dad, I took your words to heart.

I joined Kappa Delta Sorority. I'll admit it, it was more for the frat parties and less for the female friendships. But I did end up making some fabulous girlfriends with whom I still connect today, and it's like no time has passed. We did all the fun college stuff: Spring Breaks, frat parties, football games. . . . We had a lot of fun. (And made Dad proud!)

One of my favorite friends from my sorority is a sweet girl named Shelly. She has huge, natural boobs, and try as we might, they were always exposed by the end of the night. Shelly is one of the least-sluttiest girls I know. She just couldn't control her massive breasts. Her life motto was, "I'm a medium, but a small fits so cute, I wear an extra small."

During my sorority years, I lived with Shelly, two Jens, and a Laura. We also let our good friends, John and Brian, stay once in awhile when they were in between apartments. I still think it's funny that we called Brian "Grandpa" because he was like three years (or an eternity) older than us. We lived in a cute house near the sororities. I used to tell people that it wasn't in the ghetto, but the house next door was.

I got a tattoo. Just a little flower on the small of my back. But here's how I handled it with my family. I left a message on my parents' answering machine (yes, it was that long ago) letting them know what I was doing. When I returned home, forever maimed and feeling pretty, there were several messages on my answering machine:

Message 1: Mom (angry): "What did you do? How could you do this to yourself? You've only been at college for like a week. Why would you do this?"

Message 2: Dad (laughing hysterically): "I think it's hysterical. Call me and tell me all about it!"

Message 3: Kasey (pissed): "I don't understand why every time you do something stupid, I get blamed for it."

Aw yes, just the responses I wanted. Totally worth it. Of course, once I became a very professional attorney, the first thing I did was have the tattoo removed.

Oh, and it should be mentioned that around this time, Kasey and I kinda switched roles. She became the responsible schoolteacher, and I made poor decisions all through college and law school. That's right, Kasey may be teaching your children right at this very moment.

I worked a few years at Texas Roadhouse. We were the Hooters of Gainesville until there was a Hooters of Gainesville. I had no hooters. But boy, is working in the service industry fun. Definitely the best job I ever had. And I made this amazing group of good girlfriends. Do I remember those times? Not really. Were they inappropriate? For sure. If your child ever tells you that she's gotten a part-time job at a restaurant, don't be too proud. She's doing bad stuff.

When I was 21, I went with a bunch of Roadhouse girls to Mardi Gras. Of course, I decorated my car with boobs and penises and inappropriate messages for the journey up. We showed a lot of drivers our boobs. We got a huge response. It was fun.

As soon as we arrived, we glittered our tits, and hit the strip hard. We all got so many beads. We were so proud of our accomplishments. Sadly, one of my girlfriends did learn the hard, yet valuable, lesson that you shouldn't hide all your cash in your bra at Mardi Gras. One flash of those pretty glittered nipples, and you're broke.

We spent three nights in Mardi Gras debauchery. By the second night, we weren't as amused by the colorful beads. A couple of the girls, including me, had very small breasts, and the men were probably wondering why the little boys were flashing them. So we learned that we received a lot more attention if we kissed. Boys of the world, most women do this for attention, not because they're turned on, but you believe whatever you need to give me your good beads. I don't just want your circular beads. Show me your crowns, your flashing lights, your alcohol-themed pendants, your beads that resemble human sexual anatomy . . . you know what I'm talking about.

By night three, we were completely desensitized as to what is appropriate and what is not. We decided that we did not want beads at this point because our necks were starting to hurt. So we'd just willingly walk down the street, exposing our chests and kissing each other, and then when men tried to throw us beads, we were like, "No, really, keep them."

On this last night, I spent the entire time with my special partner in crime. She is a mother now and shall remain nameless, but I could write a whole book with just stories about her, and you'd be quite entertained. Once our party was over, we both went to our room and passed out. Or at least I thought we did. You can imagine our surprise the next morning, when another one of our friends, Cheryl, mentioned to my girlfriend, "That was crazy about how I found you with the maid last night." What? Huh? She was with me all night. How did she escape? My friend was equally clueless. After much debate, we surmised that this is what happened.

We entered the room and immediately passed out without even changing into pajamas or washing the glitter from our tits. A bit later, my friend awoke with a raging need to pee. Something you should know about her is that she never wore underwear. So she went to the bathroom, stumbled out of her pants, peed, and then instead of stumbling back to bed, stumbled right out the hotel door, wearing just a crop top. Luckily for her, it was close enough to morning, and a cleaning lady found her in her non-coherent, non-pants wearing predicament. Around the same time, my friend, Cheryl, was coming back to the hotel. What did she see when the elevator arrived at our floor? Our half-naked friend peering from behind a small Spanish cleaning lady. Cheryl just responded, "I've got her," and escorted her back to our room as the cleaning lady mumbled things in Spanish. You might think that Cheryl made this whole story up, but knowing our friend, not one person questioned it, even our pants-less friend. I might add that when Cheryl was telling the story, our friend still had on just a crop top.

Note to self: The tits and dicks you painted on your car for the journey up are not quite as entertaining as your hardened soul returns to the real world. They should spray Lysol at the borders to help you clean all the naughtiness away when you leave. Vegas, I'm talking to you too.

My partner in crime mentioned above eventually made a reputation for herself of being the wasted friend who pees in your bed every night. As we began to mature into young adults, this became a problem because some of us actually had nice houses and spouses to impress. So we made my friend bring a rubber mattress with her every night so that we could just rinse her and her bed down in the morning. Now, as she soon will be potty-training her first daughter, I wonder what lessons she may have learned. I would also be remiss if I didn't mention the one night we all woke up in the morning at her house, all in our own beds or couches, and found my deer friend wrapped completely under the fitted sheet in her bed. No, not the flat sheet. The fitted sheet, with all corners tucked in tightly. To this day, no one has any memory of how she got that way.

During my Roadhouse years, we often called one of my good friends "Samsonite." Why, you ask? She had taken a liking to an attractive gentleman who lived in a swanky apartment in Downtown Gainesville. It was really meant for the older grad schoolers and folks with more maturity than we had. But it was right in the heart of downtown, and this guy had money to spend. Despite all their rules and regulations, somehow, he and his buddy were able to rent an apartment in this elite building, They spent no time making a name for themselves. After about a week of late night parties, they were told that if they invited just one more guest up after midnight, they'd be evicted immediately. One might assume that they could at least sneak up a small, quiet girl. But no, this fabulous new building was on the cutting edge and had cameras in its lobbies! So every night after we went out, my girlfriend would wait outside the building as her suitor ran upstairs to fetch his Samsonite luggage. She would then crawl inside it, and he would carry her up to his apartment, in the suitcase. I always wonder about the first time she let this happen. It has "serial killer" written all over it. What's even more curious is how she exited the morning after, in more of a sober state. She still had to get in the luggage and be deposited in the street. But alas, she survived, and I will never pass a piece of Samsonite luggage without thinking of her.

And I think those are the only Roadhouse stories appropriate to tell!

"EDUCATION IS WHAT REMAINS AFTER ONE HAS FORGOTTEN EVERYTHING HE'S LEARNED IN SCHOOL."
- Albert Einstein

Never stop learning. Just because you finished high school, or tech school, or college, or grad school, or whatever, it doesn't mean that you don't have room for improvement. Whether it's staying current in your own field, or learning something completely different, learn all your life.

When I was working regularly as a lawyer, we discovered collaborative practice, an innovative approach to restructuring a divorcing family. It was so much more fair and peaceful than regular courtroom divorce. It blended with my personality so much more than litigation. So my boss and I took every course we could and became leaders in this new industry.

I've always loved fitness. So when I became a mom, I joined Stroller Strides. Within a few months, I was like, "I shouldn't just attend these classes. I should teach them!" And I didn't just want to be an instructor. I wanted to be the best instructor. I got certified and tried to give the other moms a great workout with a lot of fun included. I loved the play dates and moms' night outs. I did advanced trainings. I never stopped learning how to be the best instructor I could be.

I also became a Realtor. I learned that lawyers don't have to do much continuing education as a Realtor, so why not study and take the test? I can't tell you how valuable this new knowledge has become when buying and selling our own properties.

I have a very difficult time talking now. So my next lesson is to learn sign language and to teach it to my immediate family.

Whatever life throws at you, there is a lesson to be learned, so never stop.

LEVIN HIGH

And then there was law school. My law school adventure begins unlike any other. My college boyfriend at the time was a year older and studying for the LSAT. He was like, "I think you'd be really good at this test." I was like, "Cool, I should take it." So I took a few practice tests from his books and registered for the test. Mind you, this was after taking no prep course. I clearly didn't care that much. Perhaps my legal career was the first time I actually did something "half-assed." I took the test, and, low and behold, I got a really good score. Don't you hate me right now?

So, as the truly ambitious do, I handwrote an application to attend the University of Florida Levin College of Law. Because with my Psychology Major and Education Minor, I really didn't have another plan except continuing to party with the Texas Roadhouse crew. That's right, I applied to one school, the best in the state, and I didn't even type my application. Guess what? I got in! Crap, now I guess I had to go to law school.

And as you hoist us attorneys onto our very important pedestals, let me tell you why you shouldn't. Law school might have been more of a shit show than college. You see, budding lawyers (well, most lawyers, really) do everything to the extreme. We study hard, but we play hard too. Our "turn down" switches are broken.

Law school was more of the same as undergrad, just with a different group of friends. We did spend Thanksgivings together in Gainesville because our exams started right after the break. One Thanksgiving, we were celebrating at my friend's house. It was a wonderful evening, filled with good cheer and good turkey. Everything was fine and dandy until I decided it was time for me to go. There was a bunch of us, so we were parked all over the place, and the only way I could leave was to drive around and out from the side. So I thought. Apparently one side had a wall instead of a gradual decline like the other side. I slowly maneuvered my car down what I thought was a slope to the road, and then I heard the big bang. My car now teetered over the edge of a three-foot wall. I looked like I was making a very lazy attempt at suicide. After I got out and stopped crying, and then we all stopped laughing, we called the tow company who just hoisted my car back up over the small wall, and I let a friend drive it off the property. I think this was the beginning of my vehicle escapades. Don't ride with me unless you have a death wish.

I'm about to share with you some very inappropriate stories. Skip ahead if you're not interested. I will be using aliases to protect the guilty. Keep in mind as you read, for the most part, these people are now at the very top of the legal communities throughout the country. Just goes to show you that you shouldn't let anyone intimidate you.

A law school friend of mine wanted a shout-out in this book, and he asked that I refer to him as Hebrew Hammer. So I shall. I would like to point out that I never saw the Hebrew Hammer's penis, so I have no idea whether this name is appropriate or not. I did, however, see quite a few legal penises, not so much for sexual reasons, more so because nobody wore clothes. I wasn't actually present for this anecdote, but the Hebrew Hammer told me that on one of our first days of law school, as he was trying his best to make a good impression, he was talking with a group of peers, and he thought he was letting out a silent, non-stinky fart. As someone who is lactose-intolerant but loves cheese, this was quite the gamble he was making with his human anatomy. His body lost this bet, and he shat all down his leg.

I had another close law school friend. We'll call him the Jewish James Dean. Because honestly, that's what we called him. He had been dating a nice girl all through college, and he basically went nuts when he got to law school. He dumped her and went on what I like to consider an epic meltdown that was fun to watch and entertaining to be around. But my favorite thing about him is that he swears that his family single-handedly brought the Chicken

Dance to America at his Bar Mitzvah. Years later, he married his college sweetheart, and we did the Chicken Dance at their wedding.

One of my very best friends does not want this anecdote to be published and tells me that it's not entirely accurate. But it's really funny and how I remember it. And how do you tell your tumor friend "no"? Think Monica from "Friends," and that sums up my friend. When we first met, I called her the "Accidental Virgin." You see, she wasn't still a virgin for moral or religious reasons. She was just a virgin because she is a bit of a control freak and liked holding that power over her boyfriends' heads. Once she got to law school, she was sick of it. Not because she was so horny, but because she had lost her control. Now the boys refused to have sex with her because they knew she had waited so long, they wanted her first time to be special, just not with them. She was often like, "No, seriously, please, have my virginity, I don't want it." Only to be denied. A guy finally came along smarmy enough to take her V card, and our mission was accomplished.

I spent one law school Spring Break with two of my good friends. The guy we were with showed up to our shady motel first, and he immediately texted us, "bring your senses of humor!" It was not nice. But we didn't care. We were there for the Key West craziness, not for sleeping!

One night, my girlfriend and I decided to go home a bit early without our male companion. The cab driver politely drove us back to our motel. And then I darted out of the cab and ran. And my girlfriend had no choice but to run after me. I saw a fence, I jumped it. She jumped it. Cabby jumped it. Bushes were in the way. I hurdled. She hurdled. Cabby hurdled. I saw our room. Finally, we had made it! Except we had left our key with our other friend. We were trapped, and I paid up. When he left, my friend questioned, "Why did you make us run?" I responded, "I don't know. He charged a very reasonable fare."

Another one of my best friends was proposed to by an older law student towards the end of law school. The Accidental Virgin and I, of course, knew it was coming, so we did our best to take her out for the craziest night of her life the night before the proposal. We succeeded. She could barely get out of bed the next day. Her fiancé wanted to propose to her in the law library where they had met in a battle over his study carrel. Our sole job was to get her to take a book to him at the library where he was allegedly studying. We could barely budge her from bed. She was wearing a Victorian nightdress with lace everywhere, long sleeves, and lace turtleneck. She had makeup smeared down her face from the night before. Her hair had frizzed out to maximum capacity. We were able to get her to the library across the street while our neighbors filmed. Her response to his proposal . . . "But this is not my 'Yes, I will marry you' dress!"

Her wedding became the most celebrated wedding in history. Or at least that's how it felt to me whose friends had just started getting hitched up. She's from southern society, so she had like ten wedding showers in every city in the South, engagement parties, bachelorette parties, not to include the rehearsal dinner and wedding (to which we were late, but the reception was perfect). I was a broke-ass law student, and she wanted me to attend all her showers. So she just wrapped up the same crystal bowl each time, and we shared a conspiring look whenever it was time for her to open my gift. I never even got her the bowl to begin with!

At the very end of law school, one of my best friends was involved in a hit-and-run. Meaning that he drunkenly drove his car off a windy road and into a tree. His shoes were actually knocked off his feet during the crash. Knowing what state he was in, he ran. After all, he was just down the street from the after-party anyway. We were all there having a good old time, when my buddy ran in, looking insane, barefoot, and tried to hide under my friend's bed despite that there were storage containers under it. He was babbling fairly incoherently, but we finally got down to the truth that the cops were surely after him. Now we had bigger problems.

"Where are we gonna hide the weed?"

"Put it with the coke!"

By now, the cop lights were flashing down our door. The girl who owned the house convinced my drunk buddy that he had to walk out and turn himself in. He was going to be found anyway, and we had too much good stuff in the house for the cops to start looking for him. He did as he was told.

He took the cops to the scene of the crime. He had no real reason to not allow them to look through his vehicle, so he did. Which was fine until they got to the trunk. My friend, always a very prepared fellow, had already purchased all the alcohol for the pool party the next day. Most of it broke during the crash. So when the police opened his trunk, a mixture of liquor, beer, wine, ice, and broken glass splashed onto their feet.

"What the hell is this?!"

"It's for the pool party tomorrow, sir."

Meanwhile, I got to enjoy the 2:00 am phone call to his parents to tell them what was going on. My part of the conversation went along the lines of, "Come on, Mr. Blahblah, it's not like you've never done something like this before."

I'd also like to note that I was very close with this friend's mother. Over the years, we've drifted apart, but when she heard from her son what was going on with my health, she immediately texted me to see how I was. The problem is that her number is saved with the same contact info as her son's number. So it took me several texts to realize that I wasn't talking with my crass friend; instead, I was talking with his sweet mom. When she got all sappy on me, I told her to "stop being a pussy," thinking I was responding to her son, who tends to get over-emotional. I was not.

I also got kicked out of the Ritz Carlton. There was about a year period when I spent every bridal party at the Ritz. I got to tour the best hotels in Florida, all ending with the grand finale of eviction. I was attending my girlfriend's bachelorette party. There were about fifteen of us who all rented rooms at the Ritz and enjoyed a day at the spa, an amazing private dinner, and what was gearing up to be a fantastic night. I knew many of the girls, but some were the bride's newer friends from work. One of the girls managed to lose her clutch in the midst of all the fun. It only contained two items. . . her license and her cocaine. We scoured the Ritz looking for the bag. We did not find it. Then a very serious man tapped the girl on the shoulder and asked her to follow him. She nervously walked back with him to a room where we could all easily spy.

"Is this your license ma'am?"

"Yes."

"Is this your pocketbook?'

"Yes."

"And is this your baggie of cocaine?'

"Uh huh." (She clearly thought the good folks at the Ritz had a drug return policy. They did not.)

As soon as we heard that the police were coming to get her, we ran back up to our rooms and began launching various drugs and paraphernalia off of all our balconies. We were able to remove it all in the knick of time before our rooms were ransacked.

My very pregnant friend, who would have attended the party if she weren't about to pop, came to get my friend and me around midnight. The cocaine misplacer spent the night in jail. And the bride was proud that her bachelorette party was wilder than her soon-to-be-husband's bachelor party.

We all finally got real lawyer jobs. Most went to the State's Attorney and Public Defender offices. You have to take a lie detector test during those interviews. Apparently everyone lies while taking it, and it's no issue, unless there's something really huge lurking in your past. But my one friend just couldn't keep the truth a secret. Picture a very pretty girl, but she's acting like Sloth from "Goonies," admitting every indiscretion she's ever had.

"I mean, I have seen marijuana, well yeah, I've been around it. It may be in my system right now. Cocaine? Sure, I know it's a white, powdery substance. I may have seen my dad with some in the eighties. One time I did steal some lip gloss from a convenience store, but I was like 12. And 24. Well, it was actually lip stick in my twenties. I did cheat on a test once in high school. No, I didn't get caught, but I'd never do that again. Unless I was really sure I wouldn't get caught . . . ."

She was the only one who applied and did not get a job for the State. And she had the best grades out of any of us. She has since soared in her legal career, so we can joke about her early struggles.

Shortly after law school, one of my only friends in town was a fellow Levin High graduate, Bones. Picture a really tall, sweet guy, with no fat on his lanky bones, and too much marijuana in his already chill system. Yes, State of Florida, we are the people who represent you! Every weekend, I'd either drive to Orlando and party with my friends there, or they'd come to Tampa to hang out with us. On this particular weekend, I was excited to show off my brand new Honda Civic. Naturally, everyone went out on the town that evening, and then we planned to have an epic brunch at the Cheesecake Factory.

As everyone got ready for brunch in my meager one-bedroom apartment, Bones kept complaining that he was starving and needed MacDonald's breakfast immediately. Mind you, we were getting ready to go eat. And we weren't doing it Diva-style. We were basically washing away the filth and grime from the night before and probably puking up what remained. Finally, we had heard Bones complain and whine like a toddler enough, and I told him, "Fine, take my car to MacDonald's. But hurry up!" Bones, who does not have a hurry bone in his skeletal body, took about five minute to put on his shoes and socks, and left for his solo mission like a speeding snail. Time went by. We were all ready and starving. More time went by. Hmmm, where could Bones be in my brand new car? Eventually, about 1.5 hours into his quick jaunt to Mickey D's, he busted into my apartment, Kramer style, and said, "Oh, Lori, no. No, Lori no." I figured this was a joke, especially when my other pal, who had run down to scope out the scene, returned exclaiming, "He crashed your car!" I ran down to see my new car with a donut on one tire, and another tire about to explode.

"Looorrrriiii, noooo. A jacked-up pickup truck came from out of nowhere and ran me off the road! I had to veer into a high curb, or it would've smooshed me and my breakfast sandwich! One tire burst, and the other needed the donut. Luckily, three helpful Mexicans came from out of nowhere and changed the one tire because I have no clue how to do it. The other tire doesn't look so good." I replied calmly, "Okay, I'm glad you're okay. All this can be fixed." I was rather proud to take such a mature stance. Until my buddy opened my trunk to see exactly what the busted tire looked like, and we realized that Bones had placed the greasy, dirty tire atop my only two suit jackets. Being a baby lawyer, I could only afford a black jacket and a khaki jacket, which I kept in my trunk for my frequent journeys to the courthouse. Now they had grease stains all over them. Bones had basically ruined my only assets.

My maturity went out the window. I ranted and raved about how we all make mistakes, but it's irresponsible to make things worse when you're trying to fix your mistakes. Bones apologized profusely, explaining he would pay for my new tires and dry cleaning. After about ten minutes of attempting to load slow Bones into another vehicle so that we could actually attend brunch, we spent a lovely afternoon eating giant egg sandwiches and cheesecakes while Sears fixed my car. Bones was more than willing to treat me to brunch. To this day, he remains one of our best friends, as he shares Stewart's love of soccer (and some other stuff). He always reminds Stewart that, although they may be closer buddies now, I'm the original friend, and Stewart should never forget that. Bones remains unmarried, and we often refer to him as our third child. I do hope he gets married and has kids one day soon because I can't wait to meet the lady who could handle him and the offspring they'd create.

Our law school starting class was known as one of the worst to walk the halls of Levin College of Law. Our teachers weren't especially fond of us. We seemed to party a bit more and study a bit less than the rest of the classes. But we all ended up as lawyers in the end, so why not also be the ones who had more fun?

"'I'LL BE SPEAKING TO MY LAWYER' IS THE
ADULT VERSION OF SAYING 'I'M TELLING MY MOM!'"
- Anonymous Funny Person

What inspirational information can I give you about lawyers? Think, think, think... We're not all bad?

Seriously though, some of the best people I know are lawyers. But so are some of the worst. Isn't it like that in any profession, though? We definitely get a bad rap. Most attorneys are good people just trying to help. But before you hire one, get referrals. Ask for consultations. Do your research. Don't hire the bad lawyer. There are plenty of good lawyers out there.

And don't be overly litigious. There are absolutely times when attorneys are warranted. But not every situation. Don't try to sue someone just to get ahead. Think about the lives you will be affecting in the process, even yours. Stewart works for a huge national company whose sole goal is to determine insurance fraud. Trust me, you don't want those guys after you. Sometimes the best defense is just understanding how to act like a reasonable adult.

PILOTS AND PLANE CRASHES

So I became an attorney. I got a job at a boutique family law firm (divorce, it's really just a nice way to say "divorce attorney"). My clients would always ask me, "Wow, you must never want to get married." I'm like, "No, dumbass, I never want to get divorced." Two different things entirely.

I did think it was hysterical to put my business card on wedding presents. You know, just in case.

As a young attorney, I began to act slightly more responsible. Sure I would drive to go out, but then I'd leave my car at the valet over night, cab it home, and run to rescue my vehicle from the valet in the morning. Unfortunately, I also had a tendency to leave my keys at valets all over town, only to realize when the cab dropped me safely home, that I was now locked out of my apartment. Eventually I made ten copies of my apartment key and hid them in the dirt all around my apartment. I knew that if I just hid one, I'd never find it. So I was covering my bases. Each weekend night, you'd surely find tipsy me stumbling around in a short skirt and high heels, digging in my entryway dirt.

During this time, I dated a pilot. He was 6'6". I'm 5'2". Those differences just don't line up. I actually dated two other men around this time who were also around 6'6" tall. I don't know why I was attracting these beasts, and, I admit, I thought it was kinda cool. However, I've come to realize that more than a foot difference is inappropriate for any relationship. Anyway, let me tell you about how I met the pilot, whose name has escaped me, so we'll call him "Pete."

I was at a sushi bar (okay, it was a bar that offered like five sushi rolls late night) with my Jew Crew. It may have been late, and

I may have been drunk. I started talking with one of their friends, and we hit it off from the start. Mind you, the bar was loud, and I was drunk, so I suppose I wasn't hearing things accurately. He wore an interesting necklace with a circular pendant on it (don't get with guys who wear necklaces). I asked him about it, and here's what I heard:

> Me: That's a lovely pendant. Does it symbolize something?
> Pete: Yes. I was on the show, Survivor.
> Me (in my head to myself): OMG, I'm about to date a reality TV star! Move over Kimmy K.
> Me (casually): Oh really, that's cool.
> Pete (questioningly): I suppose.

We continued our witty banter the rest of the evening, as I dreamed of D-List fame.

The next morning, my girlfriend called to ask me if she could give Pete my number. I was like, "Um yeah, I can't believe he was on the show Survivor!" She was like, "Um, no, he's a cancer survivor." My dreams were crushed. I, of course, asked what kind of cancer it was, and it was skin. I'm like really, so he had a mole removed? Ah, the naivety of youth. We dated for about a month until I realized that he didn't shave his private parts, and it was over.

About two years later, he had a crash landing in his private plane. He and his passenger were fine, but you can bet I rode that story around for awhile, telling people the harrowing tale of how my ex cancer surviving pilot boyfriend nearly died.

Early in my career, my friend Joe and I took a much-needed vacation to Vegas, baby. After days of no sleep, run-ins with Little John and Jermaine Dupree, and more fun than I can explain, we took the redeye back to real life. About thirty minutes into the flight, all went quiet, and the plane dropped for about 45 seconds. Joe and I looked at each other, shrugged our shoulders, and made peace with the Lord, accepting our fate, while those screamed around us. Even the flight attendants. You know shit's getting real when the flight attendants react. After about 45 seconds, the normal plane noises resumed, and the plane began to coast along as if nothing had happened. There was no explanation from anyone for about twenty minutes. Then the pilot came over the intercom and said, "You might have noticed that drop. We had a bit of a miscommunication with air traffic control, and realized we were in the way of a passing plane. But we're safely cruising now." Seriously? Ever a time to lie, Mr. Pilot? How 'bout you were avoiding a flock of seagulls or something? Are you able to communicate with air traffic control now? What the bloody hell?

I think my point is that not every situation calls for the entire truth. Sure, honesty is very important, but sometimes the full truth doesn't do any good. Now, sweet flight attendant, I'll take my vodka martini so I have something to wash down my sleeping pill with. Wake me once we've crashed safely.

"THE BEST AND MOST BEAUTIFUL THINGS IN
THIS WORLD CANNOT BE SEEN OR EVEN HEARD,
BUT MUST BE FELT WITH THE HEART."
- Helen Keller

Do you find yourself in a spiral of bad relationships? I was there in my twenties, so I feel ya. I dated great guys in high school and college, but then one long terrible relationship in law school knocked me off my keister and set me on about a decade long path of dating clearly wrong men.

If you, too, find yourself in this cycle of despair, might I suggest, that the problem lies with you? Looking back, I realize that I was not ready for a good, solid relationship again, and I was putting out a vibe that attracted all the wrong types. Plus, you apparently can't find a good guy in "da club." Trust me, I researched that theory a lot.

I see a lot of women complaining on social media about how there are no good guys out there. And they list all their partner's inappropriate and unhelpful indiscretions. But there are plenty of amazing men out there. Men who will marry you and raise your children as their own. Men who will work hard to give you a good life. Men who will share your interests and explore new ones with you. Men who will buy you the Louis Vuitton and white Persian kitty 'cause you have a brain tumor. A partner is just that. . . a partner. Put more thought into choosing your life partner than your shoes for the evening. You don't have to settle for less.

Don't feel like you've wasted your time on your cruddy relationships. Think of what you've learned. If I had just had great relationship after great relationship, I wouldn't have known what to look for in a spouse. I wouldn't appreciate him as much.

And, wow, his horrible relationships really made me seem like a goddess. Helpful hint. . . date a guy who has been in lots of nasty relationships; you won't have to work too hard to keep him happy.

When you're really ready, and you find the right guy, there is nothing better.

ONLINE SHOPPING FOR MEN

I have the best husband in the world, Stewart. I mean really and truly. I can't imagine how I'd handle this situation if it were he instead of me. I don't think I could be as strong. But he's remained upbeat, optimistic, helpful, and has never made me feel strange. He calls me "My Love" everyday. I know my son will grow up to be like him, and I hope my daughter will marry someone just like him.

So how did this romance begin? Well, upon turning thirty, I told my parents that it was time I get serious and take a husband. So I began accepting every date I was asked on. I even, dare I admit, joined Match.com. It was like online shopping for men. There were a couple months when I went on two different dates pretty much every day. It was exhausting. But you'd be amazed how extravagantly men will treat you when they're trying to get up your dress. (Which they never did. I have standards. Sort of.)

And I'm the girl, so I never had to pay. Dutch, my ass. I do imagine that dating websites get pretty expensive for most men. I went in rented town cars to concerts and extravagant dinners. I brunched a lot. I met for coffee (bleh) and wine (yay). I did it all. The worst thing I did was mountain biking on MacDill Air Force Base. The coolest thing I did was deep sea fishing. The dude actually swam down, caught a fish with his bare hands, brought it back up to the boat, fileted it, and we ate it right there. (Okay, possibly he got a piece of my treasure chest, as well. But good me for not making a disgusting fish/vagina joke here.)

I even went out with a guy from the Blue Man Group. Or like a backup dancer or something. I've never seen the show. When I dumped him after brunch, he was astonished. What was he expecting? He hadn't even taken the time to paint himself blue.

77

I dated a lot of weirdos. How did I keep it all straight, you ask? I had a system. For most men, on the first date, I wore the same pink dress to the same restaurant and told the same stories. I coyly allowed them a demure kiss on the cheek at the end of the date, when I would usually promise to be in touch. Meaning, I texted them the next day that they didn't stand a chance. As an ex-waitress, I liked the idea of the staff at the Wine Exchange watching me parade in every night with a different guy and the same dress. If a fella was lucky enough to make it to Round Two, he got to see the floral floor length sundress. I had a different group of stories and restaurant for the second date, and the guy usually got a kiss on the lips, as I let him press me sexily against my house as I pretended to be way more into it than I was. Not many made it to the third date without receiving the break-up text.

My girlfriends found my dating endeavors hysterical. I may have fed off that a bit. But I kept telling them that dating is just like interviewing. It's not normal, and it takes practice. So the more dates I go on, the more ready I'll be when I finally go on my last first date.

"DON'T WALK BEHIND ME; I MAY NOT LEAD.
DON'T WALK IN FRONT OF ME; I MAY NOT FOLLOW.
JUST WALK BESIDE ME AND BE MY FRIEND."
- Albert Camus

Part of finding the right guy is not just about finding your equal, but finding someone who realizes he's your equal. Wow, that was really deep. It's true though. You need to each be proud of one another. That doesn't mean you both need to be amazing professionals, or gifted actors, or whatever. In fact, it usually doesn't work well that way. But you both must respect the role that the other plays in your relationship.

Maybe he's an ER doctor, and you stay home with the kids. So be the best damn housewife you can be. Throw those awesome dinner parties. Teach your kids a second language. Make Hubby handcrafted cocktails when he comes home from work at weird

hours of the day and do nasty things to him. I actually know a couple like this, and I love their relationship because she's like what every housewife dreams she could be. Sure, they have their moments and power struggles, but they recognize the equality of their marriage and work hard to keep it that way.

Also recognize that nobody's perfect, and we all have bad days. As the spouse, you're going to get the brunt of those. It's only natural because you're around your spouse the most. It may not be fair. And you both may not always act appropriately. But hard times will eventually pass, and good times will follow. That's life. You can't expect any relationship to only be filled with good times. You have to weather some storms to make the good times even better.

Stewart and I have really had to deal with the "in sickness and in health" part of our wedding vows over the last year. He told me just last night that his love for me is unconditional. He would rather have me in this condition than not at all. Words like that definitely make the fight easier.

MEETING THE MAN OF MY DREAMS

During this marathon of dates, I had a friend contact me wanting to know if I'd like to go to a s football game with her close friend. He had a bunch of extra tickets, had just broken up with his crazy girlfriend, and wanted to meet a nice girl. She thought we'd have a lot in common, so she made the connection for us.

It was a noon game on Sunday, so of course, we were both hungover from the night before. I'd be lying if I said I was immediately floored by him. He wore really high socks. After we chugged a bottle of champagne in his car, things got more normal. It was a really hot day, so we pretty much just walked around the inside Club Access. I liked him, but he didn't really  have me until he pulled out a picture of him and his five siblings that he kept in his wallet, and explained some crazy story about how they were all related Brady Bunch style. I thought it was really sweet how he clearly was so proud of each of them and how close they all were.

When I got home that evening and my friend asked how it went, I replied, "He's a nice guy, but it's not like I'm gonna marry him." Stewart would like me to add here that he didn't even get my number after the football game. I would like to add that I wasn't that concerned. I figured he would just get it from our mutual friend, or I would go back to dating the myriad of men who had yet to see my second date dress.

On our second date, I broke the rules and wore the first date dress. We went to a tapas restaurant, Ceviche, and he told me I could order whatever. So, I chose all veggie related items. The relationship nearly ended at this moment.

He nervously asked, "So do you not eat meat for a reason, or you just don't like it?"

"I don't like meat. I don't care if you like meat. Eat all the meat you want. I'll even make it for you. I just don't want to eat it. Because I think it tastes disgusting."

Relieved, he responded, "Oh good. Because I come from a family of cattle ranchers." I always think it's funny that a lot of the women in this cattle ranching family don't eat meat either. We grill it up for our men, and then eat our salads.

Catastrophe averted, and the date continued really well. By the end of the night, I was a bit jaded from all the weird first date "will-he" or "won't-he" have-the-balls-to-kiss-me nonsense. So, I just leaned in and gave him a kiss. It was more to get the awkwardness out of the way and less than a burning desire to put my lips on his. He stuttered, "Okay." And then we ended up sitting in his car for hours listening to music. That's how you know you've got a good one. When you just want to be around him, and he understands that it's premature to enter your domain yet. (I meant my apartment, but take whatever meaning you like.)

About two months into our relationship, Stewart flew us out with his best friend to Dallas to visit a couple of their other close friends. At this point, Stewart was my boyfriend. No, we hadn't had a discussion about it. But do people in their late twenties really need to make it "official"? We spent every night together. We had each dumped our sidepieces. And I was letting him fly me to a different state to visit his friends. Yeah, he was my boyfriend. But Stewart felt the need to really set the relationship in stone. So he officially asked me to be his girlfriend when we were in Dallas. "Do I get to wear you letterman jacket? Are we going steady?" I replied. Although the conversation seemed a bit juvenile for the mature grownups that we were, and I have ruthlessly made fun of him to this day about it, it was really sweet that this normally smooth guy felt the need to have the "talk."

As you may have noticed, I'm a pretty sarcastic, somewhat inappropriate, person. Stewart found me to be exceptionally funny, which endeared me to him more. For the first year or so, I wasn't quite sure which of his numerous friends could really hang with my jokes. So I'd constantly whisper inappropriate comments into Stewart's ear, he would think they were hilarious and repeat them, and everyone would have a good laugh. Everyone wondered how Stewart was so funny, all of a sudden. Once I got to know his friends, I became more comfortable and felt that they wouldn't be offended, and I began cracking the jokes. Now that I can no longer speak clearly, we've regressed into Stewart repeating my jokes again, but at least now everyone knows who is the source of the hilarity.

I knew he was the guy for me one day when we were grocery shopping (which come to think of it, I don't know that he has done since, at least not since I sent him for his iceberg and he returned with cabbage). I am extremely clumsy. Stewart is quite agile and coordinated. As we were walking down the aisle of tomato sauces (a clumsy girl's nightmare), I knocked a glass jar off the shelf as I reached for another. Before it hit the ground, Stewart came up right beside me and casually grabbed it as it was falling to what should have been its demise. He was like, "See, Baby, we were meant for each other."

Although, I'll never let him forget the time during a trail race when he fell on his face at the very end while the cameraman was taking his picture.

We dated for a couple years, I branded some calves. I redecorated his bachelor pad. It was the typical romance. We discussed marriage and my biological clock a lot (well, I did). And then he finally got the push he needed. His family embarks on an amazing vacation about every four years. It is one not to be missed. But you can imagine that with six children in the family, only spouses are allowed to join, not longtime girlfriends.

His stepmom knew Stewart was going to propose any minute, and she wanted me to at least be a fiancé on the vacation of a lifetime. So she gave Stewart the gentle shove he needed to propose before the trip planning. He did, and I got to spend an amazing ten days in the Grand Canyon and Sedona areas, on a hiking tour, staying in the most amazing resorts. If you know me, you know that this is the vacation of my dreams.

But apparently, my humid Florida blood doesn't handle dry climates well. I had never yet suffered a nosebleed in my life, but the faucets opened out west. There were many. I recall delicately sipping red wine near a fire pit, nibbling on cheese and crudité, as blood poured out of my nose onto my sister-in-law's pretty stiletto heel.

I love sitting in saunas, but not a good idea for this bloody girl. One day, as the resort spa was about to close, Stewart and I each went into our own saunas to enjoy some alone time. There was no one in mine, and it looked freshly cleaned, as it was closing in ten minutes. And it was white, oh so white. My robe was white, the towels were white, the room was white. I sat relaxing and enjoying my experience for about five minutes. And then the blood began to drip. Then splash. Then pour. Out of my nose and all over that clean white room. So I quickly got up and bent over to try to clean my mess as best I could. All I had was a white towel, but what could I do? You can imagine, though, that once the funnels have opened, rising quickly and immediately bending over is not a good idea. This caused even more blood to pour out of my nose. At this point, my entire white towel was a red bloody mess. So I did the only thing I could think to do. I used my beautiful white robe to quickly sop up as much as possible and ran my naked ass into the changing area. I dumped the bloody towel and robe into the clean white empty hamper and left as fast as I could. I can only imagine the reaction of the cleaning lady who had just done a marvelous job making the spa spic and span, and then returned to a crime scene.

I won't lie, I enjoy being naked in spas. When I got to experience my first "day of beauty" at a local spa, I got to try all these weird treatments I had never had before. Sure, I had had massages, facials, pedis, and manis before, but I hadn't yet been clubbed with a stone, or hung upside down, or experienced any other weird spa stuff. So during this day, when the attendant told me to get completely naked and lie face up on the table, I thought, "Sure, why not?" Except what she had actually told me was to get down to my panties and lie face down under the sheet like a normal human being. When she re-entered and asked if I was ready, I was, but she wasn't! I think she thought I was coming on to her! I wasn't, I swear, I just don't follow directions well. "Can you please pass me my panties so I can cover my cookie now?"

Back to Stewart. He's usually a pretty smooth guy. He worked as the General Manager of the biggest nightclub in Tampa in his twenties. He is currently the Vice President of Sales at a huge national company. He's outgoing and confident. But his proposal was not what you'd imagine from such a charismatic guy.

I knew the proposal was coming. In fact, in true Type A, OCD fashion, I had already designed the ring, and I knew it was somewhere in the house. Stewart had asked my dad's permission. Dad, of course, said, "Yes, take her, ha ha, she's all yours now. Don't give her back." And then months went by. Thanksgiving, Christmas, New Years, my birthday, Valentine's Day, nothing. In a passing comment once, Stewart had asked me if I would want a race finish line proposal or if I'd be mad because I'd be all sweaty in the pictures. So I made him run every race with me that year. There was even a half-marathon that friends attended, and I thought for sure that was the moment. Ran the fastest race of my life at the time. No proposal. I wore fake eyelashes everywhere. No proposal.

Then, on the last day of March (when he'd had the ring since November), we went house hunting and put an offer on a home. That night, we had a date scheduled at Ceviche (the spot of our first real date together). I'm no dummy, I was pretty sure this was it, especially when Stewart mentioned that he wanted to dress up. He was acting really strange in the car. Saying weird stuff about how I drive him and he wants to run a marathon with me.

Wiping his palms a lot. Not letting me touch his pocket (where the ring was hidden). I thought it was all pretty entertaining coming from my suave boyfriend.

When we got close to the restaurant, he really freaked out. Apparently he hadn't factored the valet into his proposal plan, and that threw him off his very smooth game. So he decided it was better to invent a story about needing to buy a birthday card for his friend. Uh huh. Whatever. He pulled into the Publix shopping area, not realizing it was just the side of the road where the supply trucks park. I pointed him towards the parking garage, where he managed to park.

He asked me to get out of the car. I was like, "No, no, no!" Not because I didn't want to marry him, but because I wanted my Ceviche proposal. I love Publix, but come on. But before I could completely resist his efforts, he was down on one knee with the ring in his hand, as people all around us loaded their sushi and laxatives into their trunks. He clearly just needed to get that ring out of his hand and onto mine. Of course, I said "yes," and off we went to our dinner at Ceviche (where I still ordered no meat).

For Stewart's wedding present from me, I wanted to have tasteful topless photos taken. How vain, right? Here's a book full of me, with whom you also get to spend the rest of your days! To be honest, it was just as much of a gift for me because I wanted to document my fabulous early-thirties body for eternity, and this was probably my only chance.

I mentioned it to my boss, and she mentioned that her husband dabbled in photography. That's right, the associate attorney tells her law firm owner attorney boss that she wants tasteful nudes, and her boss offers that her husband take them. Seems normal, right? Who would really consider this offer? That's right. Yours truly.

I spent about a month taking time off each week to go gallivanting around half-naked with my boss and her husband, each snapping photos along the way. We went to a studio and took sultry burlesque-type photos. We went out on their boat and took daytime beach photos on a private island. We went to Anna Maria Island for sunset beach photos.

The first studio shots were awkward. It was like 9:00 a.m., my boss cracked open a bottle of red, and we got started. Normally the wine drinker, I didn't want to have too much because I didn't want to look like a drunk fool in the pictures. So during each outing, my boss would basically drink a bottle of wine and end up posing for some pics herself at the end!

All my friends thought I was crazy, and looking back, it was definitely a crazy experience. But the pictures are amazing. I wouldn't have gotten such personal, diverse shots by just hiring a professional. And I always like to amuse others with my unusual anecdotes, so the story about it was almost as great as having the beautiful album of photos. For my husband. Of course. Not for myself. To this day, we still have a canvas in our bathroom of me lying practically naked on a beach. My kids always point to it proudly, and say, "Mommy!"

On our wedding day, my rancher father-in-law said in his speech that he knew I was the one for his son during that trip out west. In our travels, we saw a cow on the side of the road. One brother mentioned that he'd catch that cow. Another said he'd help pin him to the ground. The third said he'd hold the front legs. The fourth brother offered to hold the back legs. And then my sweet little voice piped up way from the back and said, "And I'll cut off his balls."

My sister-in-law also mentioned that she knew I was the one because I was the only non-blond her brother brought around the family. Note to women everywhere, dye your hair blond in your twenties and have all the fun. Then go back to a respectable and professional brunette when you turn thirty.

During family pictures on our wedding day, I thought only the siblings were taking pics at the moment. So I charmingly quipped, "And to think, all I had to do was have anal sex with him." As I heard his stoic stepmom giggle, I realized that the rest of the family had joined the picture right in time!

"LONG DISTANCE RUNNING IS 90 PERCENT MENTAL AND THE OTHER HALF PHYSICAL."
- Rich Hall

Ever wanted to run a race, but feel like you don't have it in you? Or you want to run faster, but you feel like your legs won't go any faster? I'm here to tell you, they will. Like many things in life, it just takes practice. Running is one of those sports where people get better with age. I've had many an eighty-year-old man beat me across the finish line. And I'm fast. So you can imagine how quickly he was hobbling.

Practice makes perfect. Okay, perfection is not the goal here. But if there's any achievement you want in life, you have to give it effort. You can't expect to just be the best from the start. Even if you had that high school moment where you didn't try very hard and somehow made it to regionals, those occurrences don't happen often. You need to work hard for you accomplishments, whatever they are.

Of course, people have certain natural talents that others don't. But it doesn't matter how talented you are if you don't put in the effort. And your achievements feel even better when you know how hard you worked for them.

Run, Lori, Run

My love for long-distance running began in college when one of my Roadhouse gang decided she wanted to run a race. And not just any race. . . a marathon (26.2 miles, for my non-running friends). I had never run a race in my life, but go big or go home. And all our coworkers laughed at us and told us we couldn't possibly do it, so prove them wrong, we did. If you ever want to make a good friend, train for a marathon with them. You'd be amazed at all the funny, personal stuff you share when you spend that much time alone together trying to distract one another. It took us about five hours, I cried all of mile 22, but we jogged every step. It was such an awesome feeling, and the fire was lit.

But back then, I just liked to run, I didn't care how fast or slow. I didn't care about winning. I just cared about running. So I'd happily run a nine-minute pace and enjoy my free beer at the finish line.

And then I met Stewart. He hates to run. But he loves soccer; soccer is his mistress. For about the first five years I knew him, he played multiple games a night. So, although he hated just running, he was pretty good at it. And he's a competitive guy, which turned me into a competitive girl. Soon, it wasn't just about running. It was about winning. I got faster and faster. And I won more and more. I got really fast, especially for a gal with such short strides. Think about how many more steps I have to take compared to the average-sized runner.

My last name is Skipper, and my running mantra is "Make Skippers Proud." When I get to a really mentally challenging part of a race, and neurotic counting won't help, that's what I repeat in my head, over and over. My medal holder has the mantra written across it. Stewart's competitive family has always been so supportive and impressed by my running. I know my family, too, is impressed, but I don't think they quite understand my passion and pride for it.

I decided that, considering I had run a marathon just before starting law school, I should run one before all life-changing events. So shortly after our marriage, right as we were planning to start having children, I ran another marathon. I had been cheering Stewart and his friends on the soccer field for years, so he figured there was no better chance to let them see what I could do. Around mile 25, friends and family, including my father, kept jumping out from behind trees with signs, wearing matching "Run Lori Run" shirts. The other runners around me were like, "Who are you?" It was so sweet. What a cool way to finish a race.

I've run and won hundreds of races since then, from 5k to marathon. But my biggest accomplishment happened during the marathon I ran before I became pregnant with my daughter. I couldn't understand why there was a woman on a bike filming me, who wouldn't leave my side. The race included a half-marathon, so I had no idea I was the front female marathon runner. Until about mile twelve when I  struck up a conversation with my camerawoman. Apparently I was in the lead! What motivation that was! For like six more miles. And then the female winner from the year before and former-Olympic qualifier passed me, and I couldn't catch her. I hadn't trained for more than eighteen miles, and sure enough, I could not keep up with my pace around the time when I hit eighteen miles. "Goodbye camerawoman. Nice knowin' ya. She's your girl now." Regardless, I came in second place with a 3:32:03 finish and qualified for Boston by like fifteen minutes. I was so proud. But this story displays why, if something is important to you, you should give it your all. I knew I should've trained beyond eighteen miles. But I didn't. If I had, I likely would have won the race.

I will never let Stewart live down the trail race we ran shortly after Tripp was born. Although I'm the constant klutz, and Stewart is the always agile, he managed to trip and fall on a branch at the very end of the ten-mile race, right where the photographer snaps your final photo. Obviously in my final photo, I was laughing hysterically.

Two other big wins occurred this year in 5Ks. Having just turned 40, I'm now considered a Master. I won the overall Master female at our town's giant Turkey Trot, just three months after my first brain surgery. I won my second overall Master female award during a 5k in Belleair while I was in the middle of radiation treatments.

Funny story about that Belleair 5K. . . you haven't had a Kasey anecdote in quite some time, so let's bring her back into the story. My sister came down to visit me this year and celebrate both our birthdays, which are only two days apart. Being the crazy person who I am, my favorite way to spend my birthday is to run the Belleair night 5K. It's a fun little race with a great after party with all the wine, food, and live music you could dream of.

As I've previously mentioned (boasted), I won the Masters division of this race, so I was booking it. This is no easy accomplishment when you're practically blinded by double vision and are just paying attention to the man's footsteps in front of you to assure you have a clear path. But as I was experiencing my own challenges, Kasey was struggling in a different way. Now she is not anywhere near in the best shape of her life, but she's always been a very active person, so even her "out-of-shape" is better than most people's "in-shape." I was thinking she'd probably finish in around thirty minutes. As I began to see more and more family and friends cross the finish line, I became a bit concerned. Kasey would never be the last person to finish a race. What had happened to her on the picturesque streets of Belleair?

About fifty minutes in, my concerns deepened, and more importantly, I had wine to drink and awards to win. My friends and I went to the car to change into dry clothes, and I grabbed my phone. And then I saw the texts:

Kasey officially became a runner that day. She ran the shit out of herself. I must say, I was proud. And once she got a fresh pair of clothes and a baby wipe bath, she enjoyed the after party the most out of all of us. It was the best birthday present I could've received. Oh, and Kasey granted me permission to publish this pooptastic anecdote. (Mom doesn't believe me.)

Note: Stewart has yet to run a marathon with me, despite his

promise in his proposal. I keep joking that these tumors are my friends' elaborate scheme to get out of having to run 26.2 miles with me. But y'all better at least walk a 5K in my honor.

**"BOYS WHO ARE HELD TO HIGH STANDARDS BY THEIR MOM
WILL ONE DAY HOLD HIGH STANDARDS FOR THEMSELVES."**
- Anonymous Rocking Mom of Boys

It's so important that we raise strong, yet sensitive, sons. Your son may be the cutest and brightest, but if you raise him to be a jerk, he's just that, a jerk. Raise him to be the kind of guy you'd want your daughter to date.

Have you noticed that some kids are just born a-holes? I never would've guessed it until I had my prince and princess, but I can tell pretty much from day one which ones are gonna give me problems. It's ingrained in some of them. If you have one of those, I'm sorry, do your best. And don't let them near my angels.

Let your son cry. It's okay to cry. It's okay to be sensitive. I mean, not like overly sensitive. Man up, a little. But you know what I mean. Cry when it matters. I just saw my husband cry today. It was over some serious stuff. So naturally, I poked and laughed at him.

Let your son play with the "girl" toys. I know, I know, we're all gender neutral, and there is no "girl" and "boy" stuff. But there is. Don't be surprised when your little guy dons your heels and purse. They all do that. I think. Mine did. They just want to be like their pretty mommies. But also, don't be surprised when they are drawn to the "boy" toys. I never cared what my son played with and had toys for both genders. But he always wanted to play with the trucks, trains, and robots. My daughter now has more boy toys than girl toys, as a second child of the opposite sex would, but her favorite toys are her doll babies and strollers. We haven't forced that on her. She is just drawn to more nurturing-type toys. And that's okay. Guess what? We're all just animals with instincts. And I

95

think most girls have a more nurturing instinct, and more boys have a more truck instinct.

Don't let your son feel like he deserves to win every award. He doesn't, and he shouldn't. Let him understand that he needs to work for his successes. As I keep preaching, all the gifts in the world won't get you very far if you don't have the drive to push you through.

Take my husband, for example. When Stewart was in high school, he didn't reach a growth spurt until he was a senior. So as a sophomore, he weighed only 87 pounds. There is a rule in high school wrestling that you have to weigh at least 88 pounds to wrestle in the smallest 103-pound weight class. He told his varsity cross country coaches and team that he wanted to try out for the wrestling team. They actually laughed at him! Now I can understand a bunch of high school boys laughing, but the adult coaches? Totally unacceptable, especially considering how much Stewart looked up to them. Nevertheless, Stewart tried out and made the varsity team! At one of his meets, the other school's coach tried to implement the weight rule, thinking Stewart would be too small, and his school would have to forfeit that weight class. Stewart didn't give up. He drank a bunch of water, put a bunch of coins in his pockets, weighed in fully clothed, made weight, and won! His team ended up winning the meet, but they wouldn't have if they had to forfeit Stewart's weight class. Stewart went on to be the captain of the team, a position normally held by heavy weights. He gained the team's respect and trust, and eventually, he gained some weight. Stewart is never satisfied and always wants to be number one. I feel the same way, and we are instilling that fighter spirit in our own children.

WHAT A TRIPP!

My compassionate little guy, Tripp, was our first blessing. After a year or so of trying, we were excited to be pregnant. I was already 35, so we were getting worried that it was taking so long. When we went to the doctor for my first ultrasound during my first pregnancy, there was so much excitement from the medical staff because they were feeding off of my husband's and my happiness.

I'll never forget seeing my uterus on the ultrasound. It was nearly empty. I knew immediately that this pregnancy was not viable. It took my always-optimistic husband longer to realize what was going on. At eleven weeks and four days, we learned that our first baby had stopped growing around eight weeks. I guess my body was such a hospitable environment that it wouldn't miscarry the baby naturally. We were immediately scheduled for a D&C. The emptiness that I felt after that surgery (and my miscarriages that followed) was the most difficult thing that I've ever experienced. Way harder than a mass of weird cells in my noggin.

I did receive a beautiful plant from Stewart's company to commemorate our loss. Do not send people tragedy plants. No one wants an eternal reminder of their loss that they now have to keep alive when they couldn't keep their fetus alive. We kept moving the miscarriage plant around our house where it just continued to leave dirt circles everywhere. I finally threw it away when we moved. Also, my very practical boss' response to my depressing news was, "I'm sure you figured this would happen." I know that she meant that she was sure that I knew that many first pregnancies end in miscarriages, but not appropriate. Say you're sorry, and give me a few days off!

But fairly soon after my first miscarriage, we were pregnant with Tripp. I've never been so happy in my life. I love being pregnant. I'm not good at getting and staying pregnant, but once it sticks, I'm really good at being pregnant. I honestly feel the most attractive, the healthiest, everything, once I'm pregnant. I glow. I love feeling that little monster move inside me. I think the whole disgusting experience is beautiful.

I tried for a natural birth. I'm a marathon runner. I like to push my body to do weird things. I got this.

I did not. After being in labor for about two days, I was exhausted and not making much progress. I was finally convinced that an epidural would help. The OB had written the prescription for the C-section as I finally was able to push my small, but large-headed, baby out. I do believe that he would have absolutely been a C-section if I hadn't accepted the epidural, so I have no regrets. I'm just happy that I had an amazing nurse who believed in me and let me pee all over the bed a couple times.

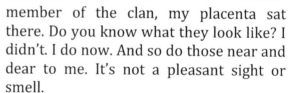

They forgot to remove my placenta. Not to say that they left it in my body, but once it was out of my body, they left it for hours on the counter of my Labor & Delivery room. I'm not one of those nuts who eat their placenta. (If you are, to each their own. I have a couple good friends who did. That's their own nasty business.) But, as my friends and family paraded in to meet the newest member of the clan, my placenta sat there. Do you know what they look like? I didn't. I do now. And so do those near and dear to me. It's not a pleasant sight or smell.

About a week after giving birth, when Tripp's umbilical cord stub had fallen off, one of my very intelligent friends asked me when I expected mine to fall off. You could tell as the words came out of his mouth, he realized how stupid he sounded. But you can't un-ring the bell. I'll never let him live this down.

Tripp is officially named Stewart Allen Skipper III. I thought everyone knew "Tripp" is a nickname for the third. Apparently not. Very good friends are astonished to this day to hear that Tripp has another name. But we all call him Tripp. I hope that never changes.

Tripp has always been an empathetic kid. He is just more connected with how others feel than most. You can't deny this quality in him. I noticed it right from the beginning. When he was around two-years old, he would get very upset watching football and yell at the players, "Why are you doing that to each other?! Stop pushing each other! Stop hurting each other!" If he sees a man who he feels is being unnecessarily angry with a woman, he's not afraid to point it out and stick up for the woman, even at age three. If he knows you're having a bad day, he's the first to give you a hug. He's got a smile and an "I love you" whenever you need one. He even offers me back rubs and gets mad if we cut his nails too short

because he likes to scratch our backs with them. He's just a really sweet kid.

Tripp is a lover of dance parties. Pretty much every night, we put on BPM music (Daddy's influence, not mine), and dance around our living room. He even dances when there's no music and when he's at friend's houses without us, and no music is on and no one else is dancing.

When he was a toddler, his favorite song was "Elvira" by The Oakridge Boys. This is more my style. He would ask to play it on repeat continuously everyday on our ways to and from preschool, and he would sing every word. He also is fond of reminiscing about how things were way back "when I was a toddler." Because now that he's five, he's apparently much more mature.

He's always been the most amazing big brother. He was so excited to see me start to look pregnant. When she was born, he was so gentle with Anna Grace and understood that he couldn't play much with her then, but soon she'd get bigger and have a blast with him. Now that she's twenty-one months and is able to interact well, Tripp always tells me, "Well that didn't take Anna Grace too long to grow big enough to play with me." Despite her mature age now, he still is always first in line to give her a hug, kiss, and snuggle. She usually responds by laughing and smacking him across the face. Sometimes he makes us feel like bad parents because he's so overprotective of her. Stewart and I are like, "Dude, chill, we got this. But thanks for pointing out that she's dancing on the counter."

Tripp's also a ladies' man. Again, from day one. He's got really good taste, 'cause he picks some stunners. And they all seem to eat him right up.

Time and time again, when given the opportunity to hang out with multiple children, he finds the prettiest little girl, and they hold hands the rest of the time. I had a bunch of my old Roadhouse gang bring their kids by the house about a year ago. Tons of kids of different genders and ages to choose from. We found him lying with a pretty little four-year old in his fancy new bunk bed with

the door closed. When we peered in to see what was going on, he quickly stood up and shut the door like a sixteen-year old.

One of my favorites is his girl, Berkley, with whom he shared a romantic year in the three-year-old program at St. James Preschool. But watch out Berks, 'cause I see your spunky little sister, Locklyn, eyeing your guy. She was just a baby when y'all met, but now she's a woman of four-years old. How will this play out?

His very best friend is Maddy, who was born about five weeks after him. On the day she was born, I brought him to the hospital, and we have a picture of them in her bassinet together. They've been inseparable since and will probably end up breaking each other's hearts repeatedly. (Don't tell Maddy that Tripp has other lady friends, 'cause she'll cut a bitch.)

Like most boys his age, Tripp is slightly obsessed with farts and poops and all things butt-related. I would be lying if I said I didn't laugh at him and encourage his booty behavior a bit. The kid's just funny.

He also went through a period when every time we passed a Home Depot, he would excitedly tell me, "Home Depot is for kids!" I have no idea what he thinks goes on inside a Home Depot. I don't even know if he's been inside one because, quite frankly, we're Lowe's people. But man, he'd be a great promoter for that place.

But what's even better than his love for Home Depot is his love for IKEA. I take him there regularly, and we make an afternoon of it. We share lunch. We walk around the showroom for hours. We play make-believe and hide-and-seek. We play with the toys in their children's section. And then we get a snack for the road and some meatballs for dinner. What mom wouldn't love a kid with a love for IKEA?

Tripp has two cows. Because what kid doesn't? Moonique and Rosita. I don't know why I feel like  sharing this. I just think it's cool. His sister's cows are Becky and Felicia. I challenge you to guess the color of each cow. I even got to  brand Felicia, and I hope one day soon to castrate one of their bull babies.

**"I JUST LOVE A SPIRITED GIRL.
SHE KEEPS YOU ON YOUR TOES AND WILL NEVER BE BULLIED."**
- Lori's Occupational Therapist

Girls. They are so cute and frightening. I feel like I can't mess up a boy that badly, but I can screw up a girl for life with just one look.

It's cause we're such forces. I'd take my uterus and vagina any day over a scrotum and whatever else they have. Actually, I'd take a penis for a little while and pee all over the place and stick it everywhere. But only for like a month or two.

Raise your girls to be strong fighters. Don't let them get pushed around by anyone. They can run the companies. They can rule the world. But they don't have to. It's just as impressive to run the household.

Stewart's sister, Victoria, has been a strong female from the beginning. Stewart's favorite story about her comes from their high school days when he was a state-ranked wrestler. A reporter was writing a piece on him and asked him how he became a wrestler. Stewart mentioned that his big sister basically beat the crud out of him all their lives and taught him how to fight. The entire article became about how Victoria paved the way for Stewart's wrestling career.

As I watch my own children now, it's like history repeating itself. Every time I post an adorable picture of my son's birthday or first day of school or other big event, the picture that gets the most attention is the one picture with Anna Grace included. People can't help themselves. And you can bet that she'll be the one teaching her calm, thoughtful big brother how to throw a punch.

I remember when I was in law school, I may have thought it was a bit pathetic that my sister was an elementary school teacher as I was about to embark on my career as an impressive high-powered attorney. But once I began to want a family of my own, I was like, "Hey, these teachers don't have it so bad. They get to earn a living while being there more with their families." I know teachers work a lot more than their school hours and earn a lot less than they deserve, but when you consider having a good family life, it makes total sense to me now.

Let your girls keep their feminine side, as well. It's fun being a girl. Pink is pretty. Sparkles are cool. We don't need to act like a bunch of frat boys. We get to do stuff like having fun at the spa and drinking too many mimosas at brunch. We can laugh and cry freely in front of others. Being a girl is awesome.

My Baby Girl (Or Neurotic Grandmother Reincarnated)

We knew we wanted another child right away. I was no spring chicken, and there was no time like the present. So we never used contraceptive, after Tripp, but I wasn't too surprised to not get pregnant immediately because I nursed for a year and hadn't yet started my period. But once the nursing stopped and menstruation resumed, another year passed with no pregnancy. I began to worry about my advanced maternal age. A good friend mentioned the luck she had had conceiving with the help of her fertility doctor and urged me to at least schedule a consultation.

Tripp was young, and I had at least three appointments each cycle, so I took him to all of them. It was okay when he was two, but as he got older, oh what that boy saw. I can't tell you how many pictures I have of him playing with a stuffed uterus.

My doctor was old school and really encouraged the least invasive intervention. So we did HCG injections and timed intercourse for over a year. I actually got pregnant! And miscarried. And got pregnant! And miscarried. It was really hard. I was taking lots of hormones, and Stewart couldn't understand why I couldn't just be happy with Tripp. I just knew there was one more baby meant for our family.

About a year into my treatments, I was standing at the waiting desk to check out, and I started reading one of the beautiful notes about how my doctor had changed a family's life. As I was coming to the bottom of the page, I read, "and that thirteen years in prison was too long. . ." And that was the end of the page, and the receptionist entered the room. I quickly paid and ran out to my car to Google what the heck was going on. I was already so invested with this doctor. He was the sweetest guy. Thirteen years in prison?!

Apparently, it was his son, not him. In the Tampa "abortion pill case," my doctor's son used his father's prescription pad and phony labels to dupe a woman to take a pill that causes miscarriages so that she'd miscarry their seven-week embryo. Mind you, the son had met this woman at a bikini bar when he was on a break with his girlfriend. My doctor ultimately gave me my beautiful daughter, so I just logged this in my brain of interesting facts about people. I am forever grateful to Dr. Welden.

Onward and upward; let's discuss masturbation. Aside from all that sexy timed intercourse (a great feat when you also have a three-year old sleeping with you), my husband's contribution was more enjoyable than mine. I'll admit that I took great joy when, early on, he had to provide a specimen to test his sperm count.

Apparently, it really goes just as hysterically as it is described in movies. Stewart was all excited. The competitor that he is, he went to the spooge office, proudly thinking, "I got this! I'm gonna break a record! I'm gonna be so fast, and my sperm is going to be so impressive!" So he goes to the office straight from work, carrying his work laptop. That's because he was working in the lobby as he waited for the good times to start, not because he can view porn from his work laptop. No problem, he had a phone. Upon seeing all these handy devices, the nurses did not offer him some nice reading material or turn on the old school porn TV located in the mandated jerk off room.

Stewart was a bit relieved when a very professional matronly older woman checked him in. He did get a little nervous, and excited, when a hot nurse came to escort him to his room. I think that's her only role at the clinic. . . hot nurse to escort men to the masturbation room. Young, pretty girls out there, apply for this position.

He entered the sterile room took the cup, shut the door, and got ready to get down to business. Only his cell phone had a low battery. Okay, no problem, he was ready to break records. He didn't need that long. What he did need was a third hand. Think about the logistics here. . . phone in one hand, penis in the other, but what to do with the important cup? Things were not off to an award-winning start. He could also hear the entire office from his special room. The only thing he could focus on was a large old school clock, ticking away his failures.

Fast forward, he somehow managed to get the job done, but disappointingly, not in record time. He left his specimen in the room and exited out the special we-know-what-you-just-did backdoor. I remember him returning home that night hoping he'd have a chance to do it again so he could be more prepared and beat his time and other things.

All the infertility issues began to take their toll on me. After two years of infertility meds and appointments, we finally bit the bullet and did a round of in vitro fertilization. I had to take a million more shots, this time mostly in my stomach. I had one of those long ice cubes that you put in a bottle of white wine to keep it cool when entertaining, and I used it to numb my skin for my shots. And then I used the wine to numb myself.

Sadly, Stewart did not get his second opportunity for public masturbation for which he was hoping. This time, he did it at home, we put it on ice, and we rushed to the doctor's office. As I was having my procedure, the embryologist came out and happily high-fived and congratulated my husband for his wonderful sperm count. I guess the doctor was used to men with very low sperm counts, so the virile nature of my husband's was exciting for them both.

Guess what? The IVF worked! We implanted two embryos and were sure we were having twins, but alas, only my strong-willed daughter, Anna Grace, survived. When the nurse called to tell me she was a girl, I responded, "Oh crap." But having a girl is so amazing. I'm so glad she's a girl now and likes pink as much as I do.

Towards the end of my pregnancy, I was telling my girlfriend that I have such a special bond with Tripp, I was concerned I may not feel the same way about Anna Grace. My friend has two kids, so I was expecting the standard "you'll love them both in different ways" discussion. Not so. She admitted that my bond with Tripp is one of the tightest she's seen, and she wouldn't be surprised if I always loved Tripp a little more! Ha, wasn't expecting to hear that! On a side note, my bond with Tripp is now just as tight, even tighter as I watch him be an amazing brother. My bond with Anna Grace is different (in the scarier, she's too smart for her own good way). But it is just as strong. And I know which child my friend clearly is bonded to more, so ha!

About a week before I gave birth, I was feeling strange and thought things might be starting to happen. So we got ready for bed early. I washed my face, went to dry it on the towel hanging in the shower, and smacked my nose straight into the wall. These are the kinds of injuries I get, with or without tumor troubles. My only real athletic injury came when I hurt my neck trying to put on a sports bra that was too tight. Needless to say, blood flew everywhere. And our bathroom is, of course, very white. So Stewart got on his hands and knees and scrubbed and scrubbed like any good man would as I bled and bled. He later told me that I better never get murdered in the house because he'll be the first suspect, and my blood splatter evidence is everywhere.

I was induced a day after Christmas. So the family needed to stay close to home for the holidays, and my stepmom-in-law was kind enough to make arrangements for the entire giant family to stay at a large house nearby. This eccentric home was actually located inside one of Tampa's beautiful nudist resorts. But it had an indoor pool, so stay we did! My son, who was just about to turn four at the time, kept mentioning how the men forgot their pants when they were walking their dogs. Stewart and I, of course, could not resist being nude, so I paraded my day-before-birth body around the neighborhood. I did wear a bra and thong, and Stewart wore his manties, so the nudists knew we weren't legit, but we had fun. (And took a lot of pics with Christmas gifts held in strange ways so that we looked naked.)

Happily, Anna Grace's birth was much less extreme than her brother's birth or her own fight for existence. The second ones really do just slip on out. Unlike the days in labor and hours of pushing I experienced with Tripp, Anna Grace's entire delivery only took about eight hours. The actual pushing part was so quick that Stewart didn't really realize what was happening until he saw the head. The doctor barely made it, commenting as he walked into the room, "Oh, she's got hair." My mother didn't have time to leave the room, so she got to watch the main event go down. She tells me that it was beautiful. And totally gross. At one point, she sat there horrified with a smile pasted to her face, thinking, "Oh my god, what is wrong with my granddaughter? What is that red thing in the center of her face?" She soon realized it was her ear, and it was right where it was supposed to be.

Anna Grace is named after my grandmother. Don't confuse her for Grandma Julie who was my dad's mom who got a bit wacked out in the end in funny ways. Like when she announced at Thanksgiving dinner that she was growing marijuana. Not to smoke. Purely because she was intrigued by how different plants grew. My uncle got to smoke it. Grandma Julie also had a bum living in her van for like a week once. I considered naming my daughter Juliana as a tribute to them both, and then I didn't.

I'll never forget my mom's response when I told her that I was naming my child after her mom. "Well, she's gonna be a spitfire." And boy, is she. From the first day, this girl has been strong. Like, physically. It was hard to change her diaper, and she was only five pounds, because she fought us so much. She has brute force.

Stewart always wanted three kids. That was the plan. Even despite my difficulties getting pregnant, he wanted to try again as soon as Anna Grace was born. I was on board, I suppose. As I was pregnant, he'd lovingly stroke my belly and talk about the third child we would eventually have. Literally as I was in the hospital, escorting a human from my loins, Stewart talked with the nurses about the third child we'd one day have. When Anna Grace was about two-months old, amidst an uncontrollable crying spell (her, not me), Stewart abruptly walked into our room, and said, "Two is enough." I haven't heard a word about a third child since.

Tripp calls her "the crazy baby." He told me a few months ago, with stress and desperation in his eyes, "Anna Grace is a sassy baby. That means she's going to be an even sassier teenager. I'm not ready for that." You and me both, Dude.

I remember when her belly button fell off or whatever it does. It didn't leave the perfect belly button I had been dreaming of. It was more like an outie. We don't have outies. I've never seen anyone in Stewart's family with an outie. What is this disgusting thing? I immediately paraded her bare belly amongst my girlfriends who all quickly agreed that it would eventually turn into a beautiful inny that my daughter could proudly display and adorn for years. All except one friend who said it might just remain an outie forever. You know who you are. Anna Grace has a gorgeous normal belly button now. I wish these were my problems these days.

She is just learning to talk, and I love hearing her little phrases. She says "Ewwww" a lot. I swear, we don't do that many disgusting things. She calls Tripp, "Tup" and Coco, "Dodo." She screams, "I want bunny!" when she wants to watch cartoons because one time she saw a cartoon with a bunny on it. (Actually, it was a donkey, but she definitely thought it was a bunny, no matter what her big brother told her.)

She also wanted to start potty training when she was nineteen-months. I'm like, "Slow your roll, girl." I have no interest in having a sorta potty-trained baby, so I'm in no rush. But whenever she has to go in her diaper, she pats it and repeats, "peepee." And then when I choose to ignore her, about a minute later, she looks at me with disgust, pats again, and says, "dirty." Stewart and my mother are much more interested in her potty training pursuits. I think it's because they didn't have to deal much with Tripp having accidents everywhere, so they haven't been traumatized like me. Whenever Anna Grace pats and says "peepee," they immediately strip her down and throw her on the toilet. Usually she ends up going. She may be ready, but Mommy is not.

Anna Grace is strong and determined, but she's also very girly. She loves her pink earrings. Her pink toenails. Pushing Dolly in her pink stroller. She does not love her bows, though, Lord, I've tried. She's loud and way too advanced for her age. I call her the "super baby" because she wasn't just accidentally created in the throws of passion like most of us. She was genetically engineered by the genius doctors who handpicked the best two embryos available, and then  she beat the other one out. That pretty much sums up Anna Grace.

With any luck, she'll have the gorgeous fashion sense of her namesake and wear high heels 'til the day she dies. She's certainly mastered Grandma Annie's spunk.

"RIGHT IS RIGHT, EVEN IF NO ONE ELSE DOES IT."
- Juliette Gordon Low

Did you know that the founder of the Girl Scouts of America, Juliette Gordon Low, was practically deaf? She couldn't start the incredible organization herself. She needed other women to help her. Many women were reluctant to assist due to their own wifely responsibilities, but Juliette was determined. When the women refused, she just pretended she didn't understand what they said. Until they agreed to help. That's my kinda woman.

Have you ever just been an ass to someone for no reason? I admit it. I have. I once was dropping off my firm's mail at the post office drive-through, and a woman walked up to it ahead of me to drop off her mail. Accidentally, only slightly, my foot slipped off the break, and I bumped her a tiny bit. Honestly, it wasn't on purpose. But she gave me a shocked look like, "How could you?" So I stared at her, and did it again, this time on purpose. She looked astonished and scurried away before the crazy lady got her. I have no idea what had come over me, but I did feel a small thrill.

There was also a woman who shared office space with us who I hated for no reason. Well, there were plenty of reasons why she was annoying, but not like hatred reasons. So I just ignored her. For years. Just pretended she wasn't in the room. For years. Never spoke a word to her. Never even acted like I knew she was there. I think that was probably quite wearing on her self-esteem. Again, I have no idea why I acted this way, and it's completely against everything I stand for. But I guess we all have our moments (or years).

My mom told me not to include these stories because I sound mean. Agreed. They make me sound mean. Because I was behaving in a mean way. And I don't condone that type of behavior. But we all have our wacky moments, and I admit to mine. No one is perfect. We are all just works in progress. Just strive each day to be better than you were the day before. And understand that sometimes, you won't.

What's my encouraging point here? Ah, yes, don't be an ass. You kill more flies with honey. We all (well, like 99% of us) have a moral compass. We know what is right and wrong. I knew I was wrong. But I just couldn't stop being a jerk to those women.

Furthermore, we are well aware when others aren't acting correctly. Don't follow the flock. If you see others out there acting inappropriately, stand up and do what you know is the right thing. You'll win the war, if not the battle.

And don't hit people with your car. It's just not nice.

KIDS DON'T MEAN THE WILD TIMES HAVE ENDED

That's right, I was the mom with the baby in the bar. I mean, they just sleep mostly at first. So why should I miss the post soccer tournament celebrations and such?

Our good times did change though. We have been on countless vacations with one family in particular. Yes, we made the kids come with us on the Disney Monorail Bar Crawl. But we also took them to theme parks and stayed at a sweet hotel, so, see, we're good parents. We've stayed several times together at an awesome resort in Orlando that has perfect activities for kids and adults. We even recently tried an excursion to Pigeon Forge, but COVID ruined that one.

We spend many more nights in, having sleepovers with good friends who are now parents of young children. It really is the best because the kids stay occupied playing with each other, AND they don't drink our wine so we get it all to

ourselves. The point is, life is even more fun when you have kids.

It was my best friend's birthday. To protect those involved, lets call her Ishelle. She has a beautiful home with a pool, and she

115

and her husband, we'll call him Jiram, are amazing entertainers. So what better way to celebrate than a day with the kids at the pool? And because it was a special occasion, we had a seafood boil as well, filled with lobster, muscles, clams, shrimp, sausage, potatoes, corn, you name it. As soon as dinner was ready, Jiram felt that he had worked hard and deserved more of a reward than just his "Jiram Juice."

Another friend stopped by with a very special birthday edible treat. Ishelle has lived a life around building a tolerance for such things, so we were not worried for her in the slightest. Jiram, on the other hand, usually is more excited by cocktails than green stuff, so we were a bit more worried for him. Of course, he is a big guy, so we figured he could hang. We were wrong.

About a half hour into his experience, Jiram got real quiet, which, if you know him, is rare. About 45 minutes in, he said, "I can't breathe, I need to go to the hospital." We laughed. We tried to get him to take a shower. Ishelle even offered him sex (on her birthday!), anything to distract him until he got over feeling too stoned and just felt drunk again. It didn't work.

Jiram finally convinced Stewart and another friend to drive him to the hospital. When they arrived, there were police parked outside. Jiram would not leave the car until the cops left because he was sure (paranoid?) that they were out to get him. After about a half hour, they finally entered the ER. When asked what was wrong with him, Jiram responded as though he was dying, "Sir, I can't breathe, you have to see me now." To which, the nurse responded, "Sir, you're talking, so you can breathe. Please sit down."

So they sat down and waited. About a half hour later, Jiram's high left him as quickly as it had arrived. He looked at his friends and said, "You're right. I'm fine. Let's get out of here." They returned home. We all laughed at Jiram. And we kept the birthday party going. No, we will never let Jiram live this down.

Stewart's brother, Jonathan, looks like Stewart's twin. Despite the three years Stewart's got on Jonathan, they pretty much always weigh the same, wear the same size and style of clothing, and have similar head hair and face hair. When my kids were babies, I always wondered if they were confused by him. Is this Daddy?

I know I was confused when I first met Stewart. Stewart and Jonathan lived together, and they'd both run around the house in the same Express manties (sexy panties for men). I found myself mistakenly checking out Jonathan on countless occasions.

We've shared many experiences together, but they became even more special when I had kids. Jonathan has always made it a point to see Tripp weekly, if not more. He even attended Tripp's first "Donuts With Dad" day at his preschool because Stewart was out of town for work. Jon made Tripp a special room with a light in the storage area under the stairs of his townhome. Tripp knows that's his spot, and there's usually a new truck in there for him.

Seven years ago, Jon met Orianna. She was only 20-years old. Mind you, I was 35, Stewart was 33, and Jon was 29. She was a baby. We even had to sneak her into bars (which doesn't work at the Hard Rock, I don't care how convincing you are). When they first started dating, there was much discussion about whether Jon could date someone so young. We quickly learned that Ori acts more mature than any of us.

Ori has become a little sister to Stewart and me. When I started having double vision, she bedazzled eye patches for the entire family to wear at Christmas. She was there in the midst of my radiation when I completed the toughest ropes course in our area that most men can't even finish. "Ori" was one of the first names my daughter could say.

Jon really found an amazing catch with Ori. She completed grad school and can hold her own with the surgeons with whom she works as a medical equipment salesperson. Oh, and did I mention she's beautiful? Not like regular-person pretty. Like possibly prettier than any person, celebrities included, who I've seen. It can sometimes be annoying to spend so much time with such a ridiculously attractive person, but it's not even a bother when someone makes a comment about her beauty, because

really, who couldn't? Oh, and she knows she's pretty, but I don't think she is aware just how hot she is. Once you get past her looks, you'd be even more impressed by her wit and charm. Don't screw this up, Jonny.

And as for my sister, Kasey, she still keeps us on our toes, but in different ways like domesticating possums and getting bug bites and rashes on weird parts of her body. She has definitely embraced her role as the cool aunt.

Our kids have only enhanced our relationships with the people we especially love. Let your children change you in positive ways, but don't change who you are at heart. Continue to let the good times roll!

**"LAUGH WITH YOUR EYES, SMILE WITH YOUR SOUL,
HUG WITH YOUR HEART, AND LOVE WITH YOUR SPIRIT."**
- Several Relevant Emojis

Nobody's future is certain. Not the healthy ten-year old next door. Not the octogenarian down the street. Not mine. Not yours.

A few months ago, I was at a friend's house where I saw his beautiful ex-wife. I was slightly embarrassed for other people to see me in my condition, especially considering how great she looked. A few weeks ago, I learned that she was admitted to the hospital with what they believe to be lymphoma and leukemia. I would have never guessed this would be her fate when I saw her very recently looking so vibrant. Just last week, I was admitted to the hospital where she is receiving chemo treatments because I was having back-to-back surgeries. Her room was actually only a few rooms away from mine! I wasn't well enough for visitors, but Stewart was sure to poke his nose in everyday to say "hello" and see if she needed anything. I know our texts back and forth during difficult times have helped me cope, and I hope they help her a little too.

I've known quite a few young people get very sick, and even die, from horrible illnesses over the past decade. I don't know if it's just that we know more people now because of social media, or if it is something in our environment. But growing up, I didn't have friends whose parents got sick or died. It just seems really prevalent now, even before it was me.

If you told me two years ago that my life would be like this now, I absolutely wouldn't believe you. When people don't understand why I don't let myself be too upset with it, it's because this could be the best it ever is again. I don't want to waste "good" times on grief.

My health conditions make it impossible for me to smile and laugh. That is probably the hardest part, not being able to show my emotions. Even when I'm at my happiest, I have no way to display it.

I know that most of my friends and family just feel sorry for me and think it could never happen to them. That's how I always felt when I learned of something horrific like what is happening to me. But the truth is, no one is immune from misfortune. You just have to do your absolute best with the hand you're dealt.

OKAY, SO WHAT HAPPENED?

I was finally living the good life. I was a lawyer for over a decade. I got my Realtor license. I became a fitness instructor for training moms while their babies come to their workouts (Fit4Mom, highly recommended). I was even the COO of a small legal publishing company. I qualified for the Boston Marathon within a year of my son's birth. Boy, was I busy. Because I did it all while taking care of my young son who has never seen a daycare in his life. I've never been so happy.

Towards the end of my pregnancy with my daughter, I began to slowly lose my voice. I didn't worry about it much, thinking it was just some weird pregnancy-related thing. And it wasn't that bad. Yet. Then I had my baby girl a day after Christmas and was so over-the-moon, I continued to ignore it.

Around April 2019, it became very bad. People could barely hear me. When I went to visit my parents, my dad made me signs to hold up that said "Yes," "No," and "F*ck Off," so that I'd have no reason to actually talk.

The tests began. Tests, tests, and more tests. My ENT finally ordered an MRI of my brain, and then we got the call. Go to the hospital immediately. You have a GIANT tumor near your brain stem. Off we went. I wasn't even surprised. I had had this feeling for years I had a tumor but thought I was just being silly and didn't want to face the fact that I could be right.

After many more tests, I learned that I had a very large meningioma near my brain stem that was growing into my nerves. It was believed to be benign, and, although large, a category one. (Is this a hurricane? Do I have the wrong terminology? Oh, well, you know what I mean. Grade, I think I mean grade.) Aside from my voice, I felt fine, so I was okay going into my first brain surgery. My girlfriends even held a "Blast the Mass" party for me!

I could have found my tumor earlier. When Tripp was about two-months old, I went to the eye doctor, and one of them noticed that my optic nerve was swollen. When I asked what that could mean, he just nervously shook his head, told me not to Google it, and sent me immediately to their specialist. His bedside manner was horrible. The specialist wanted to see me back in a few months to see if it had changed. When I returned, she said it looked the same and did not seem worried about it. My son was under six-months old at this point, and the first doctor had me so terrified that when the specialist didn't seem too concerned, and I felt fine, I didn't follow up. Looking back, that could have been the beginning of surgeries and treatments. My health may have been better for discovering it earlier, but then we probably would've missed our chance to have Anna Grace. I wouldn't give her up for anything.

After about ten hours of brain surgery on my daughter's eight-month-born-day, the craniotomy was a success. I guess. I mean, I was alive. And honestly, all things considered, I didn't feel that horrible. I jogged six days later as Stewart angrily stalked me in his car around my hood.

Going into the surgery, we assumed that they would shave off my beautiful hair. I was okay with this. I had a plan to wear lots of cute bow bands. I just didn't want to know about it before surgery. Stewart decided to shave off his hair while I was in surgery so he could meet me in recovery with the solidarity of baldness. As he was taking his razor to the hospital bathroom, he stopped a nurse along the way and asked exactly how bald I would be. Apparently not at all! They just shaved a little section near my ear! How funny would it have been if I emerged from surgery with a full head of luscious hair, and Stewart was bald?

Note to self and equally inappropriate spouse: Stop trying to joke around with your neurosurgeons. Your brain plumbers are not funny. They don't laugh no matter how many times you question them about why I still can't dance despite their fancy surgery. Stop asking them, purely for curiosity's sake, whether I was naked on the table for ten hours and how many times I farted. Joke with your ENTs. They're the funny guys of medicine, even if they can't resist sticking painful tools in your nose constantly.

About three months after surgery, I had to go back for a routine MRI just to see what was going on in my wacky noggin. Welp, that was no good and unexpected. The shell of the tumor remained, and it was "not behaving." It was continuing to grow. Not to mention, I began to experience double vision all the time. You'll never know how this feels unless you're unfortunate enough to experience it yourself.

Because of the growth, they upgraded my tumor to grade two. I was signed up for six weeks of daily radiation that ended in January 2020. And then, more waiting until another MRI could show what was happening. When we spoke with the radiation oncologist, we were happy to hear that the radiation was working to shrink the shell, and things were looking as good as they could expect. Well that's a relief.

But, honestly, I really didn't feel well. I tried to hide this from everyone because I don't think complaining helps anyone. Around Mother's Day, the left side of my face started to lose function. Mind you, my tumor was on the right side, so no one could understand why the left side was being affected. I was also having pretty severe pains in my back mostly on the left side, as well as numbing sensations in my right leg and girly parts. Oh and major balance issues. And then I lost control of the entire right side of my face as well.

Look on the bright side. . . this girl doesn't need Botox! But it's pretty hard to talk and eat when you can't move your face. I'm down from my normal 100 pounds to a whopping 80 pounds on a good day. I can't smile at my kids, kiss my husband, or joke with

123

my friends. Just the mere act of only being able to hold a perpetual frown wears on your mood. It's amazing what just being able to smile can do for you and your emotions.

We checked me back into the ER, and many, many, many more tests were ordered. But now, it's COVID era, so my hubby couldn't even stay with me. I just sat in a room all day alone in between tests. I never thought I'd get sick of "Friends." The tests showed that I have a new tumor on the left side near my ear. And I have small tumors all over my spine. I'm an anomaly. Nobody knows what to do with me.

I got to have brain surgery again! This time alone. No smiling husband to send me off or meet me when I awoke. No friends and family in the waiting room. Just me and the neuros. They took a biopsy of my old tumor, and it's the meningioma it was before, but now, an aggressive grade three. They also cleaned up the area. They assume the spinal tumors are the same as well, but I guess those neuros believe that testing those would be too dangerous. I wish I had followed that advice.

The more I deal with medical professionals, the more important I realize just how important bedside manner is. You could be delivering the same terrible news, but if you do it in a kind, concerned way and a plan to try to help, I can handle whatever it is. But if you just scare me, look at me like a freak, and tell me the prognosis is not good, I immediately close off and don't want to hear anything you have to tell me.

We just switched to Moffitt Cancer Center, which my husband jokes is the Disney of Hospitals. The employees here are very nice and do seem to care more. I started a new round of testing in the month since my second brain surgery. The doctors here decided it would be best for me to have a tumor on my spine re-sectioned and biopsied. For 24 hours after surgery, I had to lie flat on my back, right where I had just had surgery. I've never been in so much pain in my life.

I had that surgery a few weeks ago, and the spine tumors were from the same meningioma that has traveled down my spinal fluids. This is apparently a rare result. It was unlikely too that the spine surgery would cause major issues for me, but since then, I am unable to walk on my own. This girl who used to run 26.2 miles without a thought otherwise now has to use a wheelchair. I've already given myself a gnarly black eye and many bruises from falling. (Tripp does think the black eye makes me look cool, and he's not wrong.) I just started Avastin infusions and will begin radiation on my spine soon.

Because I've lost so much weight, they've also inserted a temporary feeding tube. I got to have that surgery the day after my spine surgery, so even when I was allowed to lie on my side, I had just had the feeding tube inserted, which made it nearly impossible. They say I won't survive treatment if I don't weigh more. I don't know why, but the feeding tube is really tough on me. Even the strong hit their limits.

Recovery since the second brain surgery, spine surgery, and feeding tube has proven a lot more difficult. I don't feel well. There is never a moment when I'm not in pain. I have home healthcare everyday. Just rolling across the house to my son's room is a challenge. I've lost hearing in my left ear, and there is no plan to do anything about that or the new tumor that caused it. I don't live an easy life, and I need for something, anything, to get easier.

But, at least, for now, I'm home. And there's really no place like home.

"A GARDEN OF LOVE GROWS IN A GRANDMOTHER'S HEART."
- Anonymous Sappy Old Lady

Seriously, grandmas are the best. They're all warm and sweet and squishy. They're there for you in the blink of an eye, ready to help, sometimes in an unhelpful way. But they're trying.

They will love you and your kids unconditionally. They will help any way they can. They will drink your vodka.

It doesn't have to be a grandma. Anyone from that generation who is willing to drop everything for you is an amazing person. I'm so lucky that my children have all the grandparents they do.

Learn from this generation. Their stories are important. You are their legacy. Don't let their histories die with them. Ask questions. Listen to their responses. That's how we all live eternally.

THE GRAMMIES ARE HERE, THE GRAMMIES ARE HERE!

And two of them are 4'11" and keep moving my shit. Also, turn off the light when you leave an empty room. I was not raised this way; or maybe I was.

My kids are lucky enough to have three terrific grandmothers. Abuela is Stewart's mother. She's the spunky little

Nicaraguan. She's as sweet as they come. You can't help but smile when she's around (unless you're like me and literally can't smile). She's a tad bit (really) scatterbrained. She loses her wallet or glasses or keys everyday. She takes your Tupperware and throws away important parts of your appliances. But aside from that, she's amazing. She's so good with the kids, teaching and playing with them.

Baba Gin is Stewart's stepmom. She's less emotional, but when she shows a bit of emotion, you pay

attention. She has always been fantastic with Tripp, and he has a special place in his heart for her. Dare I say, she's his favorite? Close your ears other grandmas, but I don't think you can deny that. She sends him special cards and gifts and takes him to the family ranch often. She's so patient and loving with him. It's special to watch. She's also a retired nurse, so she's been so helpful to me during my recovery periods.

Grammy is my mom. Tripp thinks she has eyes in the back of her head and finds that creepy, but loves it. My medical issues have done one good thing. They've brought everyone around the grandkids more and helped nurture their relationships. It's cool to watch your kids get close with your parents.

The grandfathers cannot be forgotten. Papa Al, aka Grandaddy, is Stewart's cardiovascular surgeon/rancher dad. He rides around with Tripp on the ranch and teaches him cool stuff like how to feed the cows and light the best bonfires. He and Baba Gin also seem to understand best when I need a good talking to abut serious medical stuff. Not pleasant, but important.

And Grampy is my dad. Tripp thinks Grampy is always grumpy. That's 'cause he is. Just kidding; that's just what Grampy tells us all. Tripp thinks Grampy has a giant brain in the back of his head. I don't know how Tripp determined this, but I got dibs on the extra brain if he's got one.

You can never tell your mom anything unless you want her to remember it for life. Which made writing this book easier. But can be troublesome in life.

I once told my mother when I was twenty that I didn't like wearing robes. I was twenty and preferred to parade my young twenty-year-old body half nude all over the house. How hard is that to understand? Now, every year, when everyone else gets robes for Christmas, I just sit and smile as my parents remind me that they would've bought me one, but they know I don't wear them. I literally would have bought several throuhout the years, but now, I suffer from Robe Rebellion. Well, guess what? I'm 41 now, have lots of tumors, no body fat, and I'm cold. I need a freaking robe. So I exchanged my mom's ugly capris for a lightweight robe the other day at Bealls. Ha. Lori for the win. Of course, when I dared to wear it the other night, it was the first thing my mom mentioned.

I just heard Stewart mention that he likes Miracle Whip on his sandwiches. He was using it in the way we call tissues "Kleenex." Like he's perfectly fine with any regular old mayonnaise, which we have. But guess what was immediately purchased and placed in my fridge? A shiny new container of Miracle Whip.

I also now know when my mom is telling a little white lie. I feel like I'm the parent and she's the child sometimes now. It's never anything huge. Just normal stuff we'd all fib about. "No, I didn't throw away pretty much all of your sippy cup inserts, rendering the sippy cups useless." "No, I didn't sneak that fresh sandwich into your house that is already so stuffed with fresh food there's no room for it." "No, I didn't run a load of laundry with just my one towel in it." "I don't know how your daughter threw all the kitty litter and poo all over the laundry room. I only left her for a second." When I hear these little fabrications, I just laugh to myself, because she says them making the same face I do when I make a small detour from the truth.

Another thing about deer old Mom that we've noticed throughout the years, she says some real obvious things. Like sometimes I just wanna respond in a super whiney twelve-year-old Lori voice and eye roll, "God Mom, I know. I'm a high-powered attorney, and I have two kids. Duh!" I'm sure she'll always think of us as our preteen selves, but as a middle-aged career woman with a husband, kids, and a serious health condition, I wasn't born yesterday and do know some common sense stuff.

For example, when I was having my first child, she reminded me several times that I would need a car seat to take him home from the hospital. "No, Mom, I was planning on just holding him in my lap in the passenger seat, old school style. Or maybe get him a nice wicker basket for the ride. What's the problem?" As we were having my daughter (second born mind you, we already had one who survived thus far to almost four!), she told me that I shouldn't put my cat in her crib, because she might smother the baby. "Um, yeah, Mom, thanks for that stellar advice. And we both know that baby ain't sleeping in that crib anyway." Or she'll tell me, in depth, how to reheat rice. As though I haven't been reheating leftovers for years.

The worst part is, as I've become a mom, apparently I've started to do it to my husband, which he loves to point out. "You sound like you mom." And I do.

RUN THE WORLD (GIRLS)

Don't worry, I researched, and I can use a song title as a chapter title. . . I know you were on the edge of your seat wondering about this. Plus, I'm pretty sure Queen B wouldn't want the bad publicity of coming after the tumor girl who was just wanting to support her inspirational song.

You'll notice a common theme in this book. I've always had strong relationships with women. Of course, I've had my share of rollicking times with the boys and can sling Jagermeister with the best of 'em, but the female relationships are the ones that will really get you through the hard times.

From the cheerleaders to sorority sisters to the Roadhouse gang to my law school ladies to the Jew Crew to my Stroller Strides tribe, women have always been at the cornerstone of my existence. I talk to girlfriends, and many are surprised that I could have so many important ladies in my life. I think many people are intimidated to start

intimate friendships. But they're so important.

A note about my Jew Crew: My mother felt the phrase needed more explanation. I thought it was pretty self-explanatory. As any good South Floridian Methodist youth should, I grew up

with a love for all things Jewish. I like their ambition and intelligence. I like their soups and deli sandwiches. So throughout my life, I've always been drawn to these Jewish folks. From best friends to boyfriends to circles of friends, I can hold my own as the only non-Jew in the room. When I discuss my Jew Crew here, it's mostly my post-law school girlfriends with whom I attended many a Christmas Eve Matzo Ball.

Not everyone needs to be your best friend. You should have a very special inner circle. But when a new friend is introduced, we should all strive to make her feel as special as the rest of your friends do when they're around you.

And not everyone needs to be a friend for life. I have scads of friends with whom I no longer hang out. Even one who lives right down the street and works with my husband. It's okay to let go of a friendship that isn't working, whether it's just situational or geographical, or you find that you just don't share the same interests any longer. No relationship leaves us unchanged. Sometimes you learn the most from those you let go. And when you're really in a bind, they do tend to come back with open arms, like no time has passed.

What Not To Say To a Sick Friend

It's really common sense, right? Ummm, no. Here's the thing, you can just say "I'm sorry." Or do little emoji prayer hands. It can be uncomfortable for people, and I get that. Not everyone is able to respond the "right" way. But if that's the case, just briefly show your support, prayers, and love. That's all you need to do. It will be remembered.

Let me digress for a second. Does anyone else laugh as much as me at the color of the emoji people make themselves on social media? Like, why are so many of us the color of the Simpsons? Or like two shades darker than we really are? Most of you are just as pasty white as the rest of us. And why do I feel like the really dark hands mean it more? They're so powerful.

Okay, so where was I? Oh yes, examples of what not to say:

1. "My neighbor's teenaged daughter was just diagnosed with brain cancer." That was it. Nothing else. No prayer for my family. No respectful sentiments. What is this, a game of one upmanship? I surrender, she wins. She's thirteen and has brain cancer. Did you happen to read my moving announcement where I indicated that mine was benign and asked for just good wishes? Now I'm compelled to worry about this family I don't even know, and frankly, I've got enough on my plate to worry about.

2. "Oh, my god, I don't think it could get any worse. Do you? I think it's really bad." I don't think I need to explain the inappropriateness of this kind of comment, especially when the sick person was very cognizant of

keeping an upbeat, positive tone and avoiding the whole "woe is me" routine.

3. Questions, questions, more questions. Okay, so just because I've just told the social media world what is going on, it's not because I really want to discuss it. Actually, it's the opposite. I'm sick of talking about it, but my family needs everyone to know that something serious is happening so they stop asking us so many damn questions. I don't want to discuss my very personal and serious health issues with most of you. I just need you to know that it's serious. Plus, we don't have answers. If you've ever really been sick, you know that it takes a long time, lots of tests, and lots of changes before decisions are made. We're not really hiding information. It just changes. All. The. Time.

4. "So how do you feel?" Well, like crap. How would you feel if you had a paralyzed vocal cord, double vision, a wonky eye, a paralyzed face, hearing loss, a numb limb and private parts, horrible back pain, two brain surgeries, radiation, spine surgery, and a feeding tube in less than a year? But do I want to complain about this? No. I'm just trying to live the best life I can while jumping the hurdles of healthcare. If I spoke to everyone about my health and how bad I feel all the time, that's all we'd talk about. If you're my husband, my parents, my sister, my best friend, you have a good idea. If you're not, and I'm not talking to you about it, there's a reason. No, I don't feel good. Ever. But what can you do? If I tell you I feel horrible, I seem like I'm complaining, which I don't think helps anyone. And if I tell you I feel fine, I'm straight up lying to make you feel better. And I need to make me feel better, not everyone else.

5. "Will you ever get better?" No probably not. Why are you making me think of these things?

6. "I don't know how you do it." Yeah, me neither. I deserve a trophy. At least a cookie. Oh, a glass of wine!

7. "Are you afraid your voice will sound like man's voice after the vocal cord implant?" Okay, this one was kinda funny. But I'd just like a voice at this point, I don't care what it sounds like.

My point is, don't make your sick friend feel even worse. Pump her up. Tell her funny jokes. Tell her she'll be fine even if you both know it's not true. And if you can't, just don't say anything.

THE VERY IMPORTANT THINGS THAT OTHERS WILL HAVE TO PROMISE YOU IF YOU'RE SICK

Okay, so this is the real reason why we all need girlfriends. I use one of those hair removal devices on my face every week. I hid this fact from my husband for years, but once he saw me push a human out my vag, I didn't really care what else he saw. But I still don't want him to feel responsible for certain beauty regimes. So, if you're like most of us women, it's time to pick a woman who you can trust to regularly shave your face. Also, if I left this to my husband, I'm sure I'd have no eyebrows. And my face-shaving attendant will likely do a beautiful job plucking my brows as well, so we kill two birds with one good friend.

Now ladies, let's get real, there are other places that need to be shaved. Lucky for me (I'm so lucky!), I vainly had laser hair removal on my girlie parts in my twenties. So I don't have much hair there. But if you do have hair there, and you can't remove it yourself, find a friend who will do it for you.

On a side note, my laser hair treatment experience was pretty funny. I remember going for the consultation, hurried as always. I rushed through the application. I got to a question about whether I've ever had a tattoo or plastic surgery. I replied that I had and went on to the next question, which included the pictures of the front and back of a woman. I quickly circled the boobs and small of the back because I had a tattoo on my back and a boob job. (Huh, what, you mean your boobs aren't just naturally huge even though you have no body fat?! No. And for the record, my implants did not cause my tumors either.)

I thought it was strange the way the consultant scurried me back to her office, shut the door, sat on the edge of her desk, and asked, "Okay, what's up?" as though I had a story to tell other than straight up vanity. After some confusing bantering, she showed me my application, and apparently, the question with the pictures was regarding where I wanted laser hair removal, not where I've had plastic surgery and tattoos. Oops. She thought I had some weird nipple and butt hair. No just normal disgusting hair in normal places. So I proceeded with my hair removal.

My boss had just completed her hair removal, so she let me use her numbing cream. So like every eight weeks, I'd go into my firm's restroom, rub down my girlie parts with my boss' numbing cream, wrap myself in a saran wrap panty which makes the cream more effective, gently walk back to my desk while making weird saran wrap noises, and wait for my appointment. Because what law firm doesn't share their numbing vagina cream?

I remember telling my family about my latest beauty treatment at a holiday dinner (where I like to drop bombs and see what happens). My mom replied, "Oh Honey, aren't you going to want hair there someday?"

"No Mom, I don't care if the big '70s bush ever makes a raging return, I will never want nasty pubes running down my leg." Oh, and my mom now waxes. You're welcome, Dad.

The point is, find close people you can depend on to do all those sick things you do for yourself on a regular basis. When you come to think of it, we all do a lot of gross stuff, so be prepared.

How To Deal When You're the Sick One

Stay busy! I know, it's so hard. You can barely move, you can barely see, you can barely hear, you can't talk, but there's always something you can do other than just lying in bed and watching television all day. I promise, that will make you sicker, both physically and mentally.

Take me for example. I began writing this book just five days after having my second brain surgery, and it will be ready to go to press within about two months of commencement. I am self-publishing, so I'm not just writing a book, I'm publishing a book, which is so much more. During that time, I've also started a blog and a website. Additionally, I've had a six-day hospital stay that included two surgeries, one major. I have double vision and horrible headaches. I have to take breaks a lot. But you know what? Staring at a TV all day would give me a headache too. So why not spend my time productively?

There's always stuff to be done. You may not be able to do a lot, but you can do something. And it's important to your occupational therapy that you do stuff. That doesn't mean that you should do it quickly or without help, but you need to get up and walk, even if it's with a walker. You need to do your different therapies. You need to do your life stuff like a load of laundry. You need to do stuff that will keep your mind from racing about what is happening to you.

Allow yourself to grieve, but do it in the ways that are right for you, not everyone else. I'm not good at grieving because I don't like focusing on negative things that I can't change. And I don't want my kids and husband to see a sad mommy all the time. I want to do whatever is best for their process. But it's not fair to have to go through whatever you're going through, and it's okay to be pissed about that.

Accept it. It is what it is, and it totally sucks. But what can you do presently to live the best life for you and your family now?

What, No Flowers?!

YES. NO FLOWERS. OR BALLOONS. When you're enjoying an extended stay at the nearest hospital, flowers can be quite cumbersome. I know that this seems unnatural for most of you. She's sick. Quick, send flowers. She will be brightened by the beautiful aromas and captivating sight.

Not so. Most hospital rooms are small and shared with a roommate. There isn't a lot of room for anything. We kinda need the one table for things like life-saving medications and food. So the flowers and balloons just keep getting moved to a new nurse station outside the room every time the patient is moved, which is surprisingly often.

And let's discuss those frequent moves. Because with flowers and balloons, you have to sit up in the stretcher and hold on to them as you glide as though in a parade to your next medical adventure. At a time when you feel horrible, motion sick, and just want to blend into the wall, the flowers and balloons atop your moving throne make you look like the Queen of England.

I know, some of you just can't resist. How about wait until she gets home, and send them there? Or even if she's not home yet, send them there for her caregivers who need tons of love, and beauty, and all those good smells too?

Better yet, let's get practical. What does she really need? Flowers that die, and balloons that deflate? Ummm, no. She and her family need useful stuff. Housecleaners. Car detailers. Games to keep the kiddos entertained. Play dates. Meal trains. Restaurant gift cards. Special nights out for the non-sick, super-stressed spouse. Cold, hard cash for her medical-related expenses.

P.S. Thank you all for the flowers and balloons.

143

EPILOGUE

There's a lesson here. I'm just not sure why I need it. I'm the nice girl. I work to build women up around me. I'm a diligent worker. I work hard for all that I have. I built an amazing life for myself and my family. So why, when all was pretty much perfect, did this have to happen? Why do I have to be everyone else's lesson?

Sometimes it's hard to not look at fat slobs and wonder why me. I know that's horrible to say, but it's the truth. I've always lived such a healthy lifestyle. I enjoy running, exercising, and eating healthy. It's hard to understand the point of a healthy lifestyle now. Because I was the healthiest one we knew. But I wasn't living that way in misery. I love those things. I really enjoy my healthy lifestyle and hope to get back to a semblance of it one day.

I come from and I've made a family of hardworking, relationship-loving people. We are not lovingly supported or financially secure because of luck. We've worked really hard. When I decided to stay home with my kids, I opened my own small law firm, acquiring my clients all on my own, and even breaking into a very niche market. I became a fitness instructor for mommies to workout with their children. I became a licensed Realtor. I even became the Chief Operating Officer of a small legal publishing company. I worked hard on developing strong relationships with others because that's important to me. My husband is the same kind of diligent, loving person I am. Those relationships we've nurtured with others through the years have helped so much now. If you don't have many of your own, there's no time like the present to work on building them. You will be rewarded when you know you're wrapped in love and support.

I have always found strength in motivating others. Whether it's encouraging moms as a Fit4Mom instructor, winning races, conquering infertility, or starting my own small law firm and real estate career after having children, I strive to be an example to others that if you are kind and work hard, you can succeed at amazing things.

People often ask me how I do it. When you're faced with no other option, then you just do it. Take each day one day at a time. When something seems insurmountable, think of those smaller challenges throughout your journey. In my experience, the big picture isn't helpful. What is helpful is knowing what the next plan is, and going from there. You just have to make it through that next rough day, or that horrible week of surgery recovery, or the months of treatments, or whatever is currently in your way. If you break a large thing into more manageable smaller tasks, you'll be amazed what you can get through. That's how I always studied for big intimidating tests. Or I tell the ladies when we're working out, you can do anything for twenty seconds, and soon enough, that twenty seconds has turned to an entire minute or beyond. This same mindset works during your major struggles as well.

This is the race for which I've been training all my life. Time will tell whether it's a sprint or marathon and whether it ends in victory or defeat.

Life's challenges are all about perspective. We can choose to be negative and defeated by even the smallest feat, or we can view the biggest challenge with optimism at the lessons that will be learned and the love that will be gained. Keep that positivity flowing, and I'll continue to set an inspiring example.

So that's it for now. I hope I motivated and inspired you. I hope you liked me, and maybe we can tour our poop books together one day. But most importantly, I hope you laughed a lot.

BOOK CLUB DRINKING GAME

Y'all knew no www.funnytumormom.com book would be complete without a drinking game. So here it is:

1. Invite all your fun friends to a party, and have everyone contribute lots of Prosecco, wine, and fancy cocktails. Don't forget your charcuterie boards, hors d'ouvres, and elegant desserts.

2. Loosen up for about an hour, discussing random things like husbands and mini-vans, gorging on all the delicious treats you've all acquired.

3. The hostess casually mentions this book, displayed on a lighted marble slab with rose petals. Begin to gush about the book and glory at its merits.

4. The hostess explains the game.
   a. Each guest gets her "funnytumormom" pin and attaches it to her dress.
   b. Throughout the night, if a guests hears another guest say "wine," "champagne," "Prosecco," or a type of wine, by region or name, the one who heard it takes the other's pin, and the wine utterer must chug what is in her glass.
   c. Also, if anyone mentions poo, she should probably use the bathroom cause she probably subconsciously has to go.

d. Once the hostess and partygoers believe that enough time has passed, the battle begins.

e. The partygoer with the most pins gets to choose against whom she'd like to play Prosecco Pong (like Beer Pong but with Prosecco and champagne flutes). It will usually be someone with no pins, but it doesn't have to be if there is a player who she feels is a lay-up. They play until one wins, and one loses. The loser drinks the remainder of the Prosecco left on the table from the game.

f. Next, the player with the most pins goes and selects the player against whom she would like to play. This continues until a bunch of losers stand around drinking, and the winners play each other until one can really claim to put the "Pro" in Prosecco.

g. The first loser pays for the winner's Uber-ride home.

Enjoy! Sorry to your husbands!

Made in the USA
Columbia, SC
20 February 2021